FIELD SPORTS LIBRARY

THE SPORTING SHOTGUN

Other Books Available

The Pheasants of The World
Dr. Jean Delacour

Pheasants and Their Enemies
Dr. J. O'C. Fitzsimons

Gamekeeping and Shooting for Amateurs
Guy N. Smith

Ferreting and Trapping
Guy N. Smith

Ratting and Rabbiting
Guy N. Smith

Hill Shooting and Upland Gamekeeping
Guy N. Smith

A Hunting Pageant
Mary S. Lovell

The Sportsman's Companion
Eric Begbie

The Notorious Poacher
G. Bedson

Famous Foxhunters
Daphne Moore

Hounds of France
George Johnston and Maria Ericson

Modern Wildfowling
Eric Begbie

THE SPORTING SHOTGUN

A USER'S HANDBOOK

By

ROBIN MARSHALL-BALL

SAIGA PUBLISHING CO. LTD.
1 Royal Parade, Hindhead, Surrey.

DEDICATION

To my wife — Shelagh

Typeset by Ebony Typesetting, West Tremabe
Nr. Liskeard, Cornwall, PL14 4LT

Printed in Great Britain by
The Garden City Press Limited,
Letchworth, Hertfordshire SG6 1JS

Published by
SAIGA PUBLISHING CO. LTD.,
1 Royal Parade, Hindhead, Surrey GU26 6TD,
England.

CONTENTS

ILLUSTRATIONS

ACKNOWLEDGEMENTS

Among the many individuals and organisations who have rendered me a great deal of advice, encouragement and assistance, I must single out the following for my particular thanks: Robert Marper, John Marchington, The Game Conservancy, Clive Wordley, John Burgess, and the arms' manufacturers who have provided me with much technical detail. A book of this type could not be written without assistance from a great many people in a variety of ways. I thank them all.

Robin Marshall-Ball

AUTHOR'S PREFACE

Despite the current recession, the bodies that represent shooting and conservation are encountering a greater number of new members than ever before. I think this is the result of three factors. The increase in leisure time has encouraged many people to take up an activity which takes them into the countryside, gives them the option of as little or as much companionship as they require, develops hand—eye coordination and physical fitness, and satisfies many of man's deep-rooted instincts in a pleasant and socially acceptable way. Shotgun shooting is a participant sport, and in these days of 'canned' entertainment, its appeal is bound to increase.

The realisation that to counterbalance shooting, the sportsman must also be a conservationist, has become increasingly accepted in recent years. Gone are the days when the shooter fired first and identified the quarry afterwards. Gone are the days when he could shoot as much (or more) as he could carry without thought to future game stocks. The time has now come when, with more and more shooters appearing in the field, each has a duty to pay (in terms of conservation) for his sport. The saying '*The best sportsman is also the best naturalist and conservationist*' should never be more applicable than now.

The final factor that has encouraged membership of shooting and conservation bodies lies in the way the sport has come under increasing pressure from those who object to it on the grounds that it is either cruel or that it is 'class–ridden'. With the danger of urban based and generally misinformed governments implementing restrictive legislation, shooters of all nations must be able to speak, through their national organisations, with a strong, authoritative, and united voice.

The shotgun user can no longer afford to be an isolated person. He should have a far broader knowledge of the stage of the sport than did his forefathers, and it was with this in mind that this book was written. When it was first suggested that I write it, I made up my mind that it should aim to provide a general background to as many aspects of the sporting use of shotguns as possible. A great many people new to shooting have plied me with questions concerning the origins of the sport, the usefulness of particular styles of guns, and many aspects of ballistics and shooting lore. Experienced shooters often seek to widen their experience and expertise by shooting further afield, and the current trend to increased leisure time has served to accelerate this process. These people, therefore, need information of the variety of shooting opportunities and whom to contact in the first instance.

I hope this book will be able to answer the questions of the novice and provide the information for the shooter with more experience. While I will be the first to admit that many points could not possibly be covered in detail in a book of this size, nevertheless I hope that it will provide sufficient to lead the reader on to seek further information and practical experience in whichever aspect of the sport that interests him (or her). If, having read this book, you find that many holes in your background knowledge have been filled, I will be satisfied. If the reader finds the book to be useful for reference on a wide range of information concerning shotgun shooting, then I will be delighted.

R.M–B.
Westbury,
Wiltshire,
England.

1

The Evolution
of the
Modern Shotgun

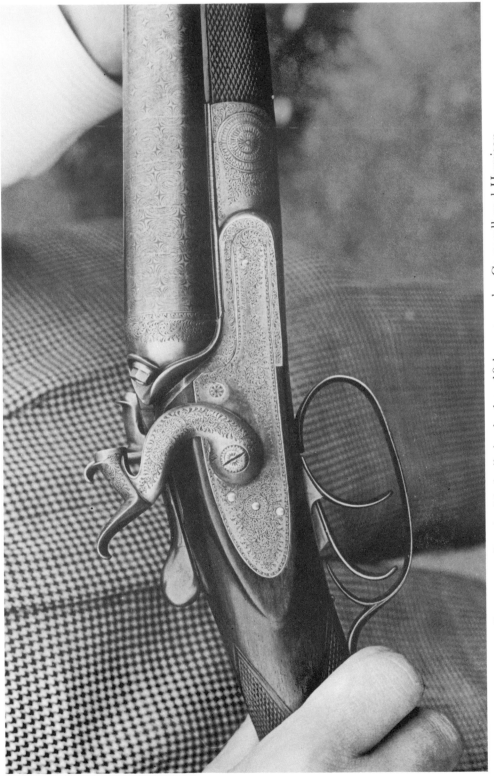

Figure 1.0   A best-quality centre-fire double built in the late 19th century by Cogswell and Harrison
Courtesy: John Marchington

The Evolution of the Modern Shotgun

DEVELOPMENT OF THE FLINTLOCK

In 1787, a patent was taken out by a certain Henry Nock which heralded the dawn of all sporting shooting, and it is from his idea that the modern shotgun, in all its infinite variety, has evolved. Most flintlock guns before Nock's time had operated on the principle of sparks, generated by the flint striking the steel, igniting powder in the pan, which in turn ignited the main powder charge through a small touch hole in the side of the barrel. Misfires were relatively frequent as there was no real way of ensuring that the powder flash in the pan would actually reach the main charge. Even if it did, the rate at which the main charge burned often depended on how well ignited it was, so velocities varied greatly. A long gun barrel was therefore essential in order to achieve a reasonable velocity as it gave the main charge time to burn properly, but this in turn made for a very cumbersome and unwieldy weapon. Certainly the early flintlock gun was one which could not be swung quickly onto a flying bird.

Nock's Gun

In Nock's revolutionary patent gun, the touch hole was positioned in the centre of the breech-plug rather than on the side of the barrel. While in no way improving the reliability of the flint ignition system, the very fact that the flash ignited the centre of the main charge meant that the powder burned more rapidly with a resultant increase in velocity. There was a reduction in the time interval between pulling the trigger and the gun discharging and this improvement gave a harder hitting, more effective weapon. Equally important, it meant that long barrels of over 40 inches (103 cm) were no longer necessary and a 30 inch (77 cm) barrel not only gave improved performance in the new gun, but also reduced the weapon's weight to such an extent that makers were encouraged to design better balanced weapons. With the increased velocity, power, and range of these lighter and better balanced weapons, bird shooting was set to move away from the stalked, close-range, uncertain shot towards the sort of wing shooting with which we are all now familiar.

Shot and Gunpowder

When considered alongside both the invention of drop-shot by William Watts in 1782 — a process which produced good spherical lead shot of uniform size — and the standadisation of gunpowder by Sir William Congrieve in 1815, it set the gunmaking trade of Britain and Europe in motion on a revolution which lasted a century. It caused such a rapid evolution of the sporting gun that guns by the greatest makers were practically rendered obsolete before they had been delivered. The revolution started from the crude long-barrelled single flintlock and ended in Europe with the hammerless sidelock ejector shotgun and, in America, with the first five shot automatic loading shotguns. By the early 1800's the sporting shotgun had been born.

The Father of Shooting

Shortly before the turn of that century, the double-barrelled flintlock shotgun had made its appearance and, despite initial opposition, the lure of being able to fire two shots at one loading was too strong. Gunmakers such as Nock, Manton, Egg, Purdey and Lancaster rose rapidly to fame as the new sport of game shooting caught on and by 1820 these people had brought the flintlock shotgun to its highest degree of perfection. The first great sportsman and sporting writer emerged in the person of Colonel Peter Hawker, though by today's standards his methods of shooting would hardly be considered sporting. One of his tactics was to pursue game on horseback until they were almost too tired to fly before resorting to his shotgun. Nevertheless, it was largely through his writings that the sport of shotgun shooting spread through Britain and her rapidly expanding Empire. With some justification he is often referred to as 'The father of game shooting'.

Guided by his teachings, the upper classes began to look upon shooting flying game birds as an enjoyable way of testing their skill with a gun. In those early days, before the advent of planned rearing of game birds, bags were small but as Lord de Grey, an eminent shot of the day wrote, 'The young gentlemen were keener and healthier sportsmen'. Birds were often shot from horseback while the loader walked beside the gun, and a number of other servants acted as beaters, dog handlers, or pickers up. Lord Malmesbury on the other hand, was reckoned to have walked a mile for every head of game he bagged, and walked-up game shooting slowly replaced shooting from horseback.

WALKED-UP SHOOTING

However, the inherent disadvantages in the design of even the best flintlock shotgun severely restricted the type of sport that could be enjoyed. It was very difficult to discharge such a gun while holding it at a high angle. As the gun was tilted the powder in the pan had a tendency to trickle out and ignition of the main charge was made even more uncertain. In addition, the time lag between pulling the trigger and the main charge of powder igniting, meant that shooting at on-coming or crossing birds was practically impossible. As a result, the new sport of walked–up shooting became well established, in which the various species of game birds and wildfowl were sought and flushed by dogs so as to present the shooter with going-away shots. The obvious advantage to a flintlock user was that the gun was rarely tilted to any marked degree and the delay in the ignition was not really critical.

By far the most profound change that these few years saw was the swing from bird shooting 'for the pot' towards a far more formal sport with a clearly defined code of practice. Game and wildfowl shooting for enjoyment and recreation had arrived, but this only affected the upper social classes. These were the people who had the leisure time for such recreation, but the standards they imposed on themselves in terms of gun safety and shooting etiquette slowly permeated the whole of the shooting society. At the other end of the social scale people who shot for the pot and for a living benefited from this upper class shooting revolution because the improvements evolved for the 'best' sporting guns of the day were soon incorporated on the cheaper weapons. At that time there was a very sharp division between the sporting, game shooting country gentleman and the yeoman pot–hunter or 'fowler, but as the industrial revolution progressed through the later part of the 19th century this division was to become less distinct.

Barrels and Design

By the 1820's the double barrel flintlock sporting gun had 30 inch (77 cm) barrels of finely twisted and carefully bored iron between which a rib had been laid along

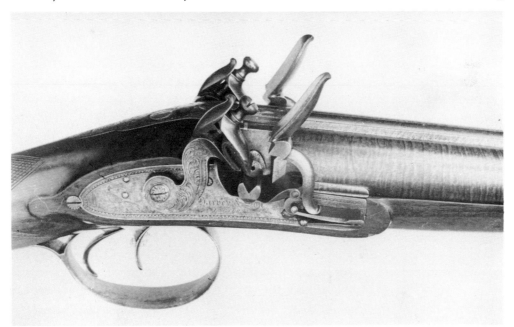

Figure 1.1   A magnificent double flintlock by Harvey and Son, showing a close up of the action and the damascus twist barrels

Courtesy: Ian Crudgington

their full length in order to assist in pointing the weapon quickly. The fore-part of the woodwork tapered rapidly beyond the action and the walnut stock had a straight hand grip. The basic shape of this gun has not changed in over 150 years of evolution to the hammerless sidelock ejector double sporting guns that are made today.

No matter how perfect or ideal any one of mankind's inventions may appear to be, if the object possesses even a slight inherent disadvantage, there will always be men who will try to seek ways to improve upon it. This is nowhere more obvious than in the shotgun's evolution in the 19th century. We have already seen that slow ignition and loose powder in a flintlock's pan were major flaws in the gun's design which many inventive gunmakers desperately sought to eliminate. In 1807 the Reverend A.J. Forsyth of Scotland devised a system whereby a fulminate of mercury could take the place of the powder in the flash-pan. This compound would ignite on being struck by a blow from a plunger and would immediately ignite the main powder charge. Within twenty or so years this invention brought to an end the long reign of the flintlock.

IGNITION SYSTEMS

By about 1825 many gunmakers had experimented, with varying degrees of success, with various devices for detonating the main charge. Following Forsyth's idea, a wide variety of ignition systems had been patented. Joseph Manton for example had designed a 'tube-lock' gun whereby a copper tube was placed in what had been the pan of the flintlock. When struck by the hammer a flame was projected sideways directly through the touch hole into the main charge. Ignition was almost instantaneous but again there were disadvantages which outweighed its merits. Other gunmakers had devised pellet-locks, and a variety of cap-ignited weapons, but after 1820 the percussion cap shotgun, in which a cap was placed on a nipple projecting upwards from the barrel, had gained almost universal approval and general acceptance. The fulminate in the cap, when struck by the hammer, projected a flash downward and forward into the centre of the main powder charge in the barrel. Ignition delay, providing the powder was dry, was almost non-existent and the new percussion cap guns could be held at a much steeper angle without fear of the cap becoming dislodged.

Percussion Cap Ignition

With this new development in the shotgun's design, bringing as it did a greater efficiency and versatility, came a new form of shooting. The fact that the gun could be fired at birds flying fast in practically any direction meant that some sportsmen took to having the birds driven towards them. Waiting at his prepared position, using two or even three percussion shotguns and assisted by loaders, the sportsman would aspire to bring the art of shooting to new heights and he would judge his prowess by the size of his bag. Although, like so many new ideas, it was initially slow to catch on, driven game shooting became increasingly more fashionable and important throughout the first half of the 19th century.

These years were really the 'Golden Age' of the muzzle-loading sporting shotgun. Many of the old flintlock guns had been converted to take percussion caps, a simple operation in itself, and the design of the muzzle loading shotgun reached its zenith. The percussion cap shotgun was the most efficient and effective weapon that it was possible to make a muzzle loader. In the time it had taken shotgun design to reach this stage, shooting as a sport had evolved from simple walked-up shooting of game and wildfowl over dogs, to driven game shooting and wildfowling in a form which has subsequently changed only very slightly. The sportsman of the early 1850's armed with his double-barrelled, percussion, muzzle loading shotgun wielded a weapon which was in almost every way as effective as a present day breech loading gun. The advances that had been made in black powder manufacture, the standardisation of shot size, and the reliability of the percussion cap produced ballistics almost equal to the cartridges of today. In addition to this, the average 19th century sportsman certainly knew more about the ballistic characteristics of his own shotgun than his present day counterpart. He knew, for instance, which particular charge of powder and load of shot best suited his gun and he would make a point of finding out which shot size threw the most even pattern from his barrels. Very few of today's sportsmen, in these days of factory-loaded cartridges, ever go to the length of finding the 'sweet shooting' loads for their guns.

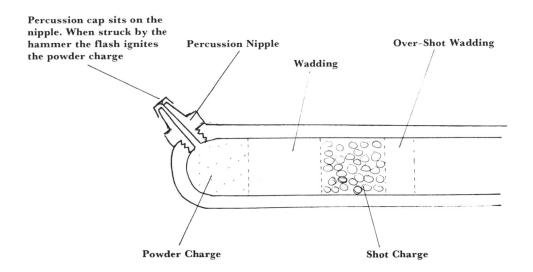

Figure 1.2   Schematic diagram of the percussion ignition system

Damascus Barrels

The double percussion shotgun of the mid 19th century was undoubtedly an effective weapon for winged game and water fowl shooting, but it had achieved something more than this. Rigby of Dublin had made the first Damascus barrels in 1818, a process by which alternating rods of steel and iron were twisted together in such a way that the barrels thus made took on a beautiful 'herringbone' pattern. This type of barrel came in to general use after about 1826 and a variety of Damascus patterns were evolved by changing the number and order of the steel and iron components. Being a stronger material than the previous 'stub iron' barrels, correspondingly less metal was needed in the barrel walls and the guns were therefore made lighter. More important though, these beautifully patterned barrels enhanced what was already a gracefully designed weapon. Gunmaking as an 'art form' as well as a skill was increasingly recognised. The two most common types of lock used in these shotguns, the 'bar' action and the 'back' action, had sufficient exposed metal to attract the attention of the gunmaker's skilled engravers. A percussion shotgun of best quality would therefore have fine Damascus barrels, highly engraved lockwork and a well figured walnut stock.

THE SHOOT

This was the era of the 'crackshot' in which the ten best game shots in the country were treated much as entertainment celebrities are today. Country estates vied with each other to produce the record bag of partridge, pheasant or grouse for the season, and the coming of the railways meant that transport to different shooting venues was a simple and quick matter. Lord de Grey and Lord Walsingham were universally recognised among the fashionable shooting circles as the people to invite to one's shoot if a record bag was to be set. More than any that went before them, they perfected the art of killing driven birds. Even in those muzzle loading days they would frequently be seen to have four birds dead in the air by taking two in front and two behind. Their loaders must have been highly trained indeed to achieve the speed of loading which enabled these remarkable men to account for so many head of game.

In order to achieve these great bags of game the techniques of game rearing and management had undergone great advances and refinements. Estates no longer relied on wild stock breeding but instituted intensive breeding and keeping programmes in order to greatly increase the number of game birds 'on the ground'. With the acceptance of the idea that it was better to drive and flush the birds in such a way as to provide the most testing shots possible, the last echoes of the pre-19th century 'pot hunting' approach died away from the grouse moors and pheasant coverts of Britain.

The shooting parties of the time were splendid and fashionable affairs lasting three or four days. The evenings would see the guns and their ladies being entertained in a lavish style and the days would see the men shooting and the ladies looking on in admiration! In such a formal setting the ladies would change their gowns four or five times a day and it was certainly not the done thing to wear the same clothes twice in one visit. Accepting an invitation to a grand shooting party would therefore involve quite considerable expense. As for the shooters, breakfast would be over by 9.30 am and the first drive would start around 10.00 am. The number of drives varied but around one o'clock the halt for lunch would be called. Lunch itself would be a meal of up to ten courses washed down by the best wines served in a marquee somewhere on the estate. The ladies would often join the party at this time in order to watch the afternoon drives, which would end around 4.00 pm. Those shooters who enjoyed the sport for its own sake must have had grave misgivings about the way it was developing. Many young gentlemen took up the sport, not because they enjoyed shooting, but because it was the fashionable thing to do, and it was this influence which led to the sport being judged purely in terms of the size of the bag.

Wildfowling

Wildfowling, on the other hand, was much more the sport of the common man. The weapons they used were larger, heavier and less finely made than those of their game-shooting contemporaries. In the rigorous conditions on the coast, where sand, mud, and salt found their way everywhere, the accent was far less on gunmaking artistry and far more on strength, the capacity to throw heavy loads of shot and simplicity of design. The coastlines of Britain and western Europe harboured a substantial number of professional wildfowlers who perfected the techniques of punt gunning, that is stalking and shooting flocks of wildfowl at rest using a large gun mounted in a frail 'punt', and foreshore shooting, whereby wildfowl were intercepted on their flight lines to and from their feeding grounds. These foreshore gunners wielded mighty weapons capable of throwing up to 4 or 5 ounces (113–142 g) of shot into the sky at any one time, but this does not detract from the fact that they were very skilled shots, their livelihood depended on their skill, and very often a killed bird meant the difference between feeding their family or going hungry. Their guns were single or double barrelled with very long barrels and were correspondingly ill balanced but, nonetheless, in the hands of a professional 'fowler it was just as effective as the finely made and balanced game guns of the gentry.

By the time the percussion shotgun had reached its peak of popularity it had brought to the world the sport of shooting flying birds in all manner of situations and conditions, by all manner of people. It had evolved a grace and elegance which in many people's opinion has not been improved upon since, and it had brought to gunmaking not only artisan skills but also artistic flair. By the very fact, however, that it remained a muzzle loader capable of being loaded only from the 'front end' it suffered two very serious drawbacks. The first of these concerned the speed at which the weapon could be loaded and the second was a safely factor when engaged in loading.

Drawbacks of the Muzzleloader

The charging of any muzzle loading shotgun is a laborious process when compared to a conventional modern breech-loader. The correct measure of powder is first poured in through the muzzle of an almost vertical gun. This is then rammed down with wadding made of a variety of material. The appropriate load of shot is then added and this is lightly rammed in order to hold it in place even if the gun, subsequently, is pointed downwards. In a percussion shotgun the gun is then primed by drawing the hammers back to half-cock before placing the percussion caps on the nipples. The hammers are then drawn back to full cock before the gun is ready for firing. Even though some of the loaders for the sporting gentry had achieved great skill in reloading quickly, the speed was still considerably slower than that we have become accustomed to in this century.

The second factor concerning safety when reloading was even more serious. It was not uncommon after a shot had been fired for a small piece of wadding to remain smouldering in the barrel. When the next charge of powder was poured in inevitably the whole lot would ignite and the flash produced would often work back to the powder flask. If the rate of shooting was relatively slow the gun barrels could of course be swabbed out, but in the heat of a driven game shoot this would be impossible and even the most eminent shots sometimes had mishaps. Lord de Grey once witnessed an incident at a partridge shoot in which Lord Walsingham's shooting butt caught fire after a spark from one of the guns ignited two powder canisters. Luckily on that occasion no-one was hurt but Walsingham and his loaders were reported to be rather singed.

Despite these disadvantages, the sportsmen of the day regarded their weapons as the pinnacle of perfection and most of the growing band of sporting writers reflected this view. The gunmakers, however, were far from complacent. The intense rivalry that existed between the eminent gunmakers in Britain and Europe ensured that the shotgun would continue its evolution. In an invention-hungry age the stage was now set for the introduction of the breech-loading shotgun.

BREECH LOADER

At the Great Exhibition of 1851, the English sporting public first had its attention drawn to a gun designed by a Paris gunmaker by the name of Lefaucheux, and a breech loading cartridge made by another Parisian, Houllier. The gun was so designed that the barrels were hinged just in front of the standing breech, and on operating the forward pointing opening lever, dropped down to reveal breech ends of the barrels, into which the cartridges were inserted. These cartridges were constructed so that when the loaded gun was closed, a pin on the base of the cartridge protruded from the top of the barrels. When the pin was struck by the hammer it ignited the fulminate inside the base of the cartridge and the gun fired. The first pinfire shotgun and cartridge had been made.

To the twentieth century shotgun user the advantages of this system over the percussion muzzle-loader are obvious, but at the time the great majority of gunmakers viewed this new-fangled weapon with considerable scepticism. W.

Greener, in his book *Gunnery in 1858* mounted a blistering attack on the French breech-loading system, stating that in almost every way the breech-loader was inferior. The great majority of these criticisms were undeniably true, the breech-loader was certainly heavier than its muzzle-loading counterpart, the recoil was greater and the system of locking the barrels closed was a weak point in the design. In addition the Lefaucheux gun threw inferior patterns, needed more powder per charge and its cartridge had a tendency to stick in the chamber after it had been fired. What Greener, and others like him, failed to realise is that every new invention inevitably suffers from teething troubles and he did not stop to consider the potential of the weapon, blinded as he was by superficial faults.

Joseph Lang had the opposite view. He had the foresight to see this development as a significant advance in shotgun design and within the year he was selling his own version of the gun. At the time the percussion muzzle-loader was unquestionably the better gun except where it came to the speed and safety of re-loading, but the balance was slowly tilting in the favour of the breech-loader and within ten years all Greener's criticisms could be discounted. The introduction and slow acceptance of the pinfire brought about such a storm of controversy that *The Field* conducted a series of tests which reflected the fact that as the design of the breech-loading gun was improving so its performance came to equal that of the muzzle-loader. With its additional advantages of quick, easy and safe loading, the breech-loading gun was here to stay.

Other gunmakers such as Lancaster, Westley Richards, and Leetch devised their own form of breech-loading shotgun but by 1860 due to its simplicity of design, the

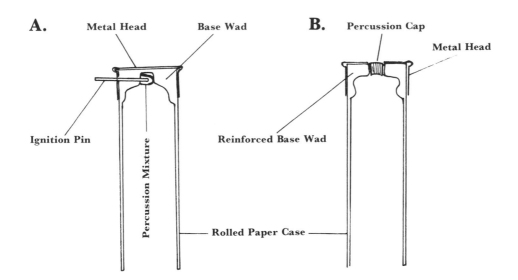

Figure 1.3   Cartridge Cases:
      A. Pinfire cartridge case   B. Daw's centre fire cartridge case

pinfire shotgun was eventually accepted by all the important gunmakers. Many of them made advances which cured the weaknesses of the original Lefaucheux gun. Such gunmakers as Dougall, Westley Richards and W. W. Greener strengthened the action and the mechanism which locked the barrels. Others eliminated the early pinfire's annoying feature of having to be half-cocked before the gun could be opened. Needham's side leaver mechanism of 1862 half cocked the hammers and opened the gun in one movement. Gas-tight cartridges were evolved to cure the rather disconcerting habit of exploding gases escaping past the pin when the gun was fired. Cartridge extractors were incorporated into the gun which made the extraction of the spent cartridge so much easier.

By 1865 the design of the breech-loading, pinfire shotgun had been perfected, but its acceptance had been so slow initially that comparatively few of the famous gunmakers ever produced them in quantity. One disadvantage of the pinfire system had, however, been impossible to cure. By the very fact that a rather large pin protruded from the base of the cartridge, any rough treatment of the ammunition was liable to cause an explosion. The pinfire cartridge was vulnerable and it was this factor only which caused the pinfire shotgun, with its elegant back action locks, to fall quickly from favour when an efficient centre fire gun and cartridge was designed and brought into use. Despite its rather brief history, the pinfire was nevertheless an important stage in the shotgun's evolution as it firmly established the ascendancy of the breech-loader over the muzzle loading gun.

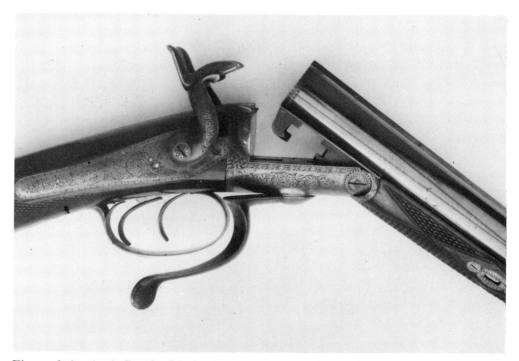

Figure 1.4   A pinfire double by J. Dickson. Note the under-lever and the angle at which the hammers are positioned in order to strike the vertical pins
Courtesy: Ian Crudgington

CENTRE FIRE GUN

The history of gunmaking in the late 18th and 19th centuries seemed to take on a definite pattern. Relatively long periods of calm, when a generally accepted type of weapon was slowly improved and eventually perfected, were followed by shorter periods of frantic activity as the various gunmakers tried to capitalise on some new idea. So it was after Forsyth's invention that a decade of hectic gunmaking experimentation and innovation produced a wide variety of ignition systems before the percussion cap emerged as the accepted norm. Similarly, when the first successful breech-loading shotgun was developed there followed a decade of experimentation with a variety of ignition systems before the centre fire cartridge, based on Daw's patent, emerged. During the period between 1855 and 1865 the gunmaking trade in Britain and Europe was in a turmoil. Double percussion muzzle-loaders for the die-hard traditionalist were being produced alongside pinfire breech-loaders and the gunmakers' own patent centre-fire guns. Never before or since have individual members of a shooting party brought together such a wide variety of guns. In a typical shooting party of eight guns one would probably find three sportsmen using pairs of muzzle loading percussion guns, perhaps another three using pinfire guns, and the other two sporting a 'Needle gun' or a 'Lancaster base-fire' gun. The mixture certainly reflected the frantic pace at which the gunmakers were advancing the designs of their weapons.

The makers realised that the centre-fire gun possessed a number of distinct advantages over the pinfire. Apart from the safety factor concerning the pinfire cartridge, loading the gun was slow, as each round had to be correctly aligned with the pin uppermost when loading it into the chamber. In addition, despite improvement in the design of the cartridge, there was always a risk of hot gases blowing back past the pin close to the shooter's face. The centre fire system, therefore, brought with it quicker and safer loading and much easier storage of the ammunition. As early as 1852, Needham produced a centre-fire weapon in which a long thin needle pierced the base of the cartridge and detonated the fulminate. The 'Needlegun', as the weapon came to be called, had double barrels but they were fixed in a manner reminiscent of the muzzle-loader. Its action gave it the appearance of a double-barrelled bolt action gun but differed in that the bolt swung outwards in the Needham gun rather than backwards as in a true bolt action. While the system enjoyed a brief popularity, its slow loading, ungainly appearance and rather odd cartridge meant that it was quickly superceded by subsequent developments.

In the same year as Needham's gun appeared, Charles Lancaster also designed and produced a centre-fire shotgun which was years ahead of its time. The cartridge was fired by striking the centre of the metallic base, beneath which lay a detonating mixture on a fixed perforated disc. The flash from the mixture escaped through the perforations into the main charge. The cartridge base had a rim which facilitated reloading as it engaged on extractors which moved out from between the barrels as the gun was opened. The one drawback of Lancaster's 'Base-fire' system was that the ammunition was expensive and less readily available than that of the pinfire. Though it never caught on, it certainly gave an indication of what was to come.

In 1861 George Daw introduced the cartridge in which the percussion cap was sunk centrally in the base of the case and this type of ammunition has remained unchanged to this day. The case was designed originally in Paris by Pottet, copied and improved by Schneider and presented to the British sporting scene by Daw. Because of this mixed origin, Daw failed to get the patent rights and this undoubtedly was a contributory factor in the rapid acceptance of the cartridge. Within a very short time gunmakers were producing a wide variety of weapons using the new centre-fire ammunition. With all the experience of pinfire breech-loading design to draw from, strong, efficient and elegant centre-fire shotguns were produced very soon after the first introduction of the ammunition.

Although most pinfire shotguns were back action weapons, the centre-fire gun was increasingly made in bar-action, that is, with the main spring forward of the hammer rather than behind it as in the back action. Between 1865 and 1880 with the standardisation of the cartridge, the double barrelled hammer gun was gradually improved and refined. One of the inherent weaknesses in all breech-loading shotguns lay in the manner in which the barrels were locked to the breech when the gun was closed. Some of the early breech-loaders certainly had a tendency to work loose and many of the gunmakers sought a really secure method of fastening the barrel to the action. One significant advance was the 'bolt' designed by Purdey whereby a metal bar sprung into slots on the lump beneath the barrel when the gun was closed. Westley Richards designed a weapon in which the

Figure 1.5   Two types of centre-fire 12 bore hammer guns — a top-lever double and an under-lever single

barrels were held secure by a rearward extension of the top rib and, eventually, most gunmakers settled for a combination of these locking devices.

'Action' and Levers

The method of opening the gun also led to a variety of designs. Lefaucheux's original breech-loader had a forward pointing underlever which swung sideways to open the gun. As the breech-loader became more popular, underlevers which pointed backwards towards and over the trigger guard appeared, as did sidelevers. These levers were not sprung, so the gun had to be closed manually by closing up the barrels and then returning the lever to its locked position. This could still take too long if grouse, partridge or pheasant were being driven in large numbers at the sportsman and this caused the evolution of the self locking or 'snap action' guns. From the designs that have come down to us from that time it would seem that a spring operated opening level could be placed practically anywhere on the gun's action, but eventually the underlever, sidelever and thumblever gave way to the top lever which became, and still is, the most widely used method of opening a double-barrelled shotgun.

Barrels

By this time also, Damascus twist barrels were slowly being replaced by those made of steel. The advances made in steel refining technology meant that good

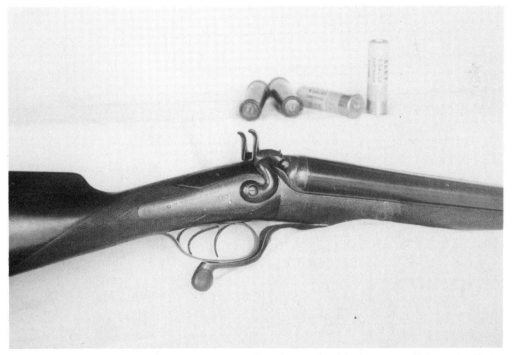

Figure 1.6   Wildfowling gun — an under-lever double hammer 8 bore built in England in the late 19th Century by William Moore and Grey

quality metal was more easily available and cheaper than ever before and though there was initial opposition to steel barrels from the gunmaking and shooting fraternity, as with all other innovations, they became accepted as they were proved to be reliable in use. Although there was no denying that, for sheer beauty, the subtle and graceful patterns of a Damascus barrel could not be matched, or that when compared to steel the Damascus barrel tended to bulge rather than burst if a blockage occurred, barrels made of steel could be forged more cheaply and with greater efficiency than those made of Damascus twists. This consideration, while not influencing the traditional sporting gentry, certainly was of significant importance to the sportsman in the new rising middle classes in a Britain and Europe in the midst of their industrial revolutions.

In 1866 a method of boring the barrels in order to reduce the spread of shot was developed and this quickly became known as choke boring. In a choke-bored barrel the internal diameter was effectively decreased towards the muzzle and the effect of this was to concentrate the pattern. Killing shots could therefore be taken at greater ranges and, after the convincing demonstrations mounted by *The Field*, Britain was swept by a wave of enthusiasm for heavily choked guns. However many sportsmen soon realised that this method of barrel boring, which was attributable to both Pape and Greener, had its own draw-backs. The more a bore was constricted, the more were individual shot crushed and deformed and this, in extreme cases, caused a deterioration in shot pattern. Also, the small spread of shot at the normal driven game ranges meant that the birds received so many shot as to be unfit for the table. A decade after its introduction gunmakers were producing heavily choked long range wildfowl guns and lightly choked game guns. A sense of perspective had returned.

HAMMERLESS SHOTGUN

When we consider that by the 1870's, the cartridge, barrels, woodwork and barrel bolting mechanism had evolved almost as far as they could, the only step forward that could now be taken was to eliminate the external hammers in favour of an action that was totally enclosed — the so called hammerless shotgun. There were many arguments for and against the desirability of developing an internal hammer action for a shotgun. An external hammer was a graceful adornment on a gun when it was carefully forged and engraved and had the additional advantage of enabling the shooter to tell instantly if the gun was cocked and ready to fire or not. On the other hand, each hammer had to be manually pulled back to full cock every time the weapon was to be fired and this was considered by some to be time consuming. There was also an ever present danger of the hammer catching on some article of clothing, being inadvertantly pulled almost to full cock and then released. Such accidental discharges led some manufacturers to seek ways of bringing the hammers into the body of the lock and, in 1871, Murcott in London produced and marketed the first hammerless action gun to achieve any degree of success. His gun had an underlever which, on being pushed down and forward, cocked the internal hammers and opened the gun. The locks were of a modified side-lock pattern and the gun had a snap action. With its clean and graceful lines and good balance the gun was an instant success unlike the earlier attempts at a hammerless gun by Daw in 1862 and Greener in 1866. The popularity of Murcott's gun which, because of the noise it made when being cocked and fired came to be known as the 'mousetrap', posed the first serious threat to the total dominance of the hammer gun.

Many other designs of hammerless action were patented and each achieved a certain degree of success but the most important development came in 1875. Anson and Deeley, two of Westley Richards' workers, designed a 'boxlock' hammerless action. Within the year Westley Richards was marketing guns built to Anson and Deeley's design. With the combining of a number of separate parts of a conventional side-lock action into fewer components, the action they designed was simpler, stronger and above all cheaper to make. Other manufacturers, particularly of the cheaper guns, were quick to adopt the boxlock action and by 1880, the evolution of the British and European double barrel sporting gun had reached a stage that has since remained basically unchanged.

Most double barrel hammerless guns of this period were built with the barrels arranged side-by-side, but shotguns with the barrels superimposed were also developed. By the turn of the century, the best London gunmakers could produce either side-by-side or over and under shotguns of the highest quality, craftsmanship and reliability in a form which has not changed to this day.

AMERICAN SHOTGUNS

By 1880, the rapid expansion and settlement of the North American continent both north and south of the U.S.A.-Canada border had caused the emergent American gunmaking industry to evolve a distinctly American design of shotgun. Up until the late 19th century, the gunmaking industry of the New World had played a very secondary role to the European guntrade in shotgun development, while it led the world in rifle development and design. The European design of shotgun, the double-barrel hammer, and later hammerless, would be pressed into service in the new type of wing shooting that was slowly evolving in North America, but there were some fundamental characteristics of the European gun which made it less than ideal for this new role.

The American shotgun user often found that he had to survive on what he shot. His shooting was undertaken in remote areas far from any repair facilities for his weapons, so the design of the gun had to be both strong, and simple to maintain. In addition, it must be remembered that the United States was a comparatively poor nation at the time and the expensive imported double shotgun was beyond the reach of many hunters. The most popular style of shotgun which had evolved in Europe at the time was a rather light game gun which could occasionally be pressed into service using heavier loads against wildfowl. In America, conditions seemed to demand the opposite, that is, a heavier gun for use with heavy loads against waterfowl but retaining the capability of being used against upland game as well. In all these matters, the European gun, being as it was rather more delicate than the rugged conditions demanded, expensive, and open bored, was not the ideal weapon for the American hunter.

The large scale emigration of Europeans to America in the latter half of the 19th century did mean, however, that the double gun was sure of a market in the New World. Bringing with them as they did the European preferences in their choice of sporting guns, such American gunmakers as L.C. Smith and Colt produced large quantities of both hammer and hammerless double shotguns to meet their demands. It was not until the late 1880's that the true American shotgun began to emerge. Lacking the traditional skills of their European counterparts, the American gunmakers also found that there was a huge home demand for shotguns which could not be satisfied by craftsmen and custom built shotguns. With admirable enterprise the pioneering gunmakers sought ways to simplify the shotgun design in order to increase output. Aligning the two barrels in a double gun is both time consuming and costly, so the American shotgun reverted to one barrel. In order to retain or even increase the potential fire-power of the weapon the makers devised ways in which the gun could be made to fire more than one shot at a loading, and the repeating shotgun was born. In addition they brought assembly line techniques to the craft of gun making and the production of these new single-barrel repeating shotguns at last began to satisfy the demands of their domestic market. The guns had to be reliable, simple to operate and maintain, heavy enough to cope with long-range loads, and cheap. The repeating and later automatic loading shotguns that were thus evolved, filled these demands admirably.

Repeaters and Autoloaders

One of the earliest of these repeating shotguns was produced by Winchester. Known as the 'Winchester repeating shotgun' its design was derived from the famous Winchester lever action repeating rifles. It had a long tubular magazine beneath the barrel which contained up to five cartridges, and with another already loaded into the chamber the gun had a six shot capacity. Reloading was accomplished by throwing the combined trigger guard and lever forward, an operation which ejected the fired cartridge case, returning the lever to the stock and chambered another round ready for firing. This gun was in production in 1888 but, while the mechanism was eminently suitable for rifles, the shotgun design encountered a number of problems and it was soon superceded by more efficient reloading systems.

In 1890, the United States President Mackinley introduced a tariff on imported guns which was to be the starting point of the American gunmakers' rapid expansion. This tariff of over 35 per cent on each weapon imported reduced the fierce foreign competition for sales on the American continent and enabled the American arms' manufacturers to break away from the task of competing with the imported arms. In their search for the ideal shotgun many designs of repeating mechanisms were tried, achieved limited success and were then abandoned until, just after the turn of the century, John M. Browning patented an automatic loading shotgun. He designed a weapon which utilised the recoil to blow the bolt

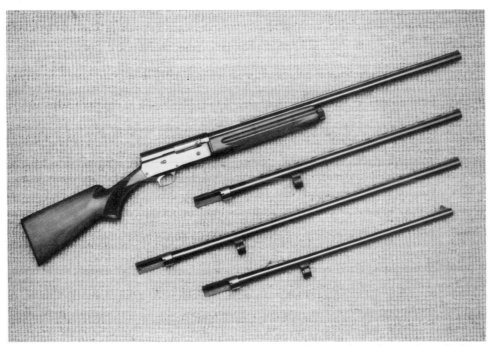

Figure 1.7 First reliable autoloader — descendant of a pioneering design. This five shot Browning recoil auto has remained virtually unchanged in over 75 years

back, eject the spent case, and load a new one from the under-barrel magazine, in one rapid if violent movement. Ironically Browning first offered his gun to a number of American gunmakers but after many refusals, sold the licence to a European maker, Fabrique Nationale in 1902. Thus the first really classic American autoloading shotgun was made initially in Europe. In the very traditional sphere of British and European game shooting, the new auto-loading and repeating American guns were considered very inferior weapons but it is highly significant that Browning's five shot recoil automatic shotgun has not needed any modifications in about eighty years of manufacture.

Pump Action

The other type of repeating shotgun to emerge as the classical American gun was the pump action. Instead of allowing the recoil to reload the weapon, the wooden fore-end of a pump gun is manually slid to the rear after a shot has been fired, to eject the cartridge case, and slid forward again to reload. Whilst seeming clumsy at first, reloading can be a very rapid process and in the hands of an experienced shooter a pump gun can be a formidable weapon. Remington produced the first really successful hammerless pump action gun in 1907 and it was designated as their "Model 10". Winchester marketed their Model 12 pump action shotgun from 1913 onwards, and both these models bear a very close resemblance to the weapons that these companies and others manufacture today.

THE MODERN GUN

It had been barely a hundred years since the Reverend Forsyth designed his fulminate of mercury ignition system which brought about the decline and fall of the flintlock gun, and only about fifty years since the first breech-loading shotgun had begun to gain grudging acceptance, but by the first decade of the 20th century the styles of shooting, the guns, cartridges and calibres had been standardised at a stage that has not changed since. The British and European double barrel sporting gun had evolved along the lines of traditional design and craftsmanship, and the 'New World' expansion and settlement had caused a vastly different type of shotgun to be evolved to answer the needs of the young continent. It has to be admitted that some types of gun have undergone slight modifications or improvements but more often than not these are changes in style to suit a change in consumer taste rather than any fundamental change in the workings of the gun. In barely a century bird shooting for sport and recreation had become firmly established and the sporting gun had emerged from the flint firearms of the late middle-ages to the modern weapons we are all familiar with today.

2

Lock Stock and Barrel —
Shotgun Shooting Jargon

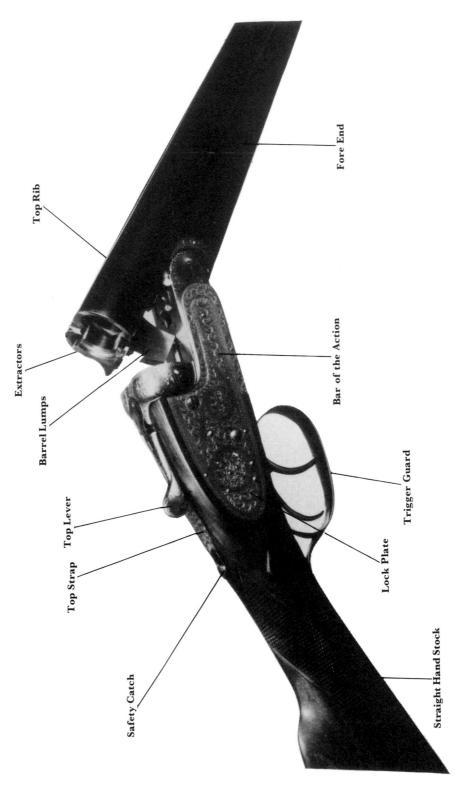

Figure 2.0   Close-up anatomy of a double-gun
Courtesy: Churchill, Atkin, Grant & Lang

Top Rib

Fore End

Extractors

Barrel Lumps

Bar of the Action

Top Lever

Top Strap

Trigger Guard

Lock Plate

Safety Catch

Straight Hand Stock

Lock Stock and Barrel — Shotgun Shooting Jargon

Every interest, sport or pastime that people indulge in generates a whole new vocabulary of specialised words or phrases. To a person entering a new activity, be it stamp collecting, chess, or shooting, this specialist vocabulary can be both confusing and frustrating, particularly if he sees that even 'experts' on the subject interpret the terms differently. To complicate matters further many countries have different names for the same objects so that now, in these days when a home gun market is also flooded with imported guns, some sort of international cross reference is needed. In this chapter I hope to be able to give the novice some of the idea of the meanings of the specialist jargon most often used and to explain some of the principles behind the workings of the shotgun and cartridge ballistics.

CALIBRE AND BORE SIZES

To a person who has never been involved in shotgun shooting, even the city dweller who has never seen or handled a shotgun, the words '12 bore' will bring mental identification of the weapon as a shotgun. What would perhaps surprise him is the variety of other calibres of shotgun that are available, each with their own advantages and disadvantages and each suited to a particular type of shooting. In terms of popularity of course, the 12 bore gun is the leader by a long way, but those people on the fringe of the shooting scene will also know that the 20 bore and the .410 bore are shotgun calibres with their own strong following of devotees. The other, lesser known, shotgun calibres remain very much as unknown quantities even to many people who are ardent shotgun users.

Bore Number

There are, at the present time, nine calibres of breech-loading shotgun that are used in the various kinds of sporting disciplines available in Britain, Europe and North America, but before I go on to describe them in detail I must explain how these calibres came to be so called. The bore number of the gun denotes the number of lead balls exactly fitting the barrel which went to one pound in weight. Therefore, a gun that fired a lead ball weighing four ounces would be called a '4 bore' and one whose lead ball weighed $\frac{1}{20}$ lb would be called a '20 bore'. It can be seen then, that the smaller the number, the bigger the gun, but there are two exceptions to this rule in that the two smallest shotgun calibres are designated by the measurement of their bore diameter in inches or millimetres. In Europe and North America the word 'bore' has been supplanted by the word 'gauge' but in most countries these words are interchangeable. Therefore '12 bore' and '12 gauge' mean the same thing.

The nine calibres in use today are as follows: 4, 8, 10, 12, 16, 20, 28, .410, and .360 or 9 mm. All, with the exception of the .360 (9 mm) use a centre-fire paper or plastic cased cartridge based on Daw's centre-fire design, and the .360 inch gun fires a rim-fire 'Flobert' type cartridge in which the firing pin strikes the rim of the cartridge base to ignite the percussion mixture. Other calibres of breech loading shotguns have been produced in the past but even before World War II the 14 bore, 24 bore and 32 bore became obsolete as the supply of ammunition dried up. These guns are now either collectors' pieces or else they have been re-chambered and bored out to take a more readily available cartridge. In a similar manner cartridges for the 4 and 8 bores are now in very short supply, but in Britain at least, these calibres will continue to be used by a small minority of sportsmen who have resorted to loading their own ammunition.

Figure 2.1   Cartridges for large bore guns — European wildfowling calibres. *Left to right:* 4 bore, two 8 bores, 10 bore, 12 bore *(for comparison)*

4 Bore Shotgun

Although, at one time, 2 bore shotguns were made in small numbers and were wielded by powerful men as shoulder guns, the 4 bore is now the largest shotgun which is still in use.

These mighty weapons were usually built as single barrel guns for shoulder use and double barrel for use as a mounted gun on a boat or punt. Even the single barrel gun weighs close on 20 lbs (5 kg) and could only be swung easily by a muscular and well built shooter. These guns averaged 40 inch (1 m) barrels and usually had the underlever locking mechanism, which was both strong and simple. The last 4 bore was probably built in the early 1920's as, after that date, they became increasingly uneconomical to use due to the general rise in the cost of making both the guns and cartridges.

As a shoulder gun capable of shooting birds, especially waterfowl, at long range it had no equal, and it was the most powerful weapon in the coastal wildfowler's armoury between the two world wars. Although designated a 4 bore the load of shot per cartridge averaged between 3-3½ oz (85-99 g) and this was loaded in cartridge cases 4 inches (10 cm) long. In a well bored gun this would be capable of throwing killing patterns up to a maximum of around 80 yards (73 m). Some of the English gunmakers specialised in making large bore guns of this type and nowadays their products are becoming increasingly valued as collectors' items. Guns by such makers as Bland, Tolley, Holland and Holland and Greener produced during the heyday of wildfowling on the coasts of Britain and Europe from 1900 to 1930 were built to withstand the extremely rugged conditions they encountered and a surprising number have survived to this day.

These great wildfowling guns were usually built using the back action and external hammers, and the hammerless 4 bore is a very rare gun indeed. In the rugged conditions in which these guns were used, the additional complication and cost of a hammerless action was not easy to justify to the professional 'fowler or market gunner. In the depression of the early 1930's the days of these professional hunters all but came to an end and the guns which, because of the spiralling cost of cartridges, became uneconomical to use were quickly discarded and found their way into the armouries of the growing band of amateur waterfowl shooters.

Nowadays, with one 4 bore cartridge costing as much as fifty 12 bore cartridges, the 4 bore user is, understandably, sparing in the use of his big gun. In addition to these financial constraints there are legislative restrictions on the use of this calibre. In many countries of Europe and in the U.S.A. and Canada the use of this gun against live quarry is forbidden. Even in Britain, traditionally the home of these wildfowling calibres, more and more wildfowl habitats are being closed to big gun users. This is a pity in many respects as a 4 bore user is far more likely to be thoughtful about the type of shots he takes than an indiscriminate 12 bore gunner with a plentiful supply of cartridges.

8 Bore Shotgun

Similar legal restrictions apply to the 8 bore. This calibre, considered by many to

Figure 2.2   An 8 bore single hammer under–lever by Holland and Holland: in the
               past many best quality gun makers also made such large bore 'fowling
               guns

be the ultimate in wildfowling weaponry, is the second largest calibre still in use. 8
bores were made in a great variety of styles and configurations from single barrel
hammer guns, with barrel lengths up to 50 inches (127 cm) to double barrel
hammerless guns with 36 inch (91 cm) tubes. This diversity in design also gave rise
to great variations in the gun's weight, but the sweetest shooting 8 bore averaged
between 12 and 15 lbs (5.44–6.9 kg). As with the 4 bore the great majority of these
guns were built with external hammers and an unsprung rotary underlever
opening mechanism, but there were a substantial number of other designs and even
hammerless single and double barrelled 8 bores were made in small quantities.

Although originally bored to take a spherical lead ball weighing two ounces (57
g), the 8 bore was developed progressively to fire heavier loads. The standard gun
was chambered for the $3\frac{1}{4}$ inch cartridge loaded with two ounces of shot, but from
the early 1900's to about 1930 when the last 8 bores were built, guns were
chambered for a variety of cartridges up to the 8 bore magnum case of $4\frac{1}{4}$ inches
shooting up to $2\frac{3}{4}$ (79 g) of shot. In addition, 'chamberless' guns were built to fire
thin walled brass cartridges instead of the paper cartridges and this wide
diversification eventually contributed to the rapid decline of the 8 bore as the
depression of the early 1930's began to take effect. Ammunition makers soon
abandoned the brass cases and magnum cartridges to concentrate production on
the 'standard' load, and even this cartridge rapidly became more costly to produce.
Though to a lesser extent, the 8 bore suffered the same decline as the 4 bore as the
numbers of professional wildfowlers declined.

In Britain, at any rate, the attraction of using a large calibre gun, such as the 8 bore, has brought about a faint revival of interest in this weapon. Within the last few years I have seen a muzzle-loading 8 bore produced for the British market by an Italian gunmaker and the discovery that the Remington Industrial cartridge cases are made in 8 bore size has brought about a surge of interest in 8 bore reloading. Although to my knowledge no 8 bore breech-loading shotguns have been produced since the 1930's, I have recently heard of two instances of Spanish 10 bore double barrel hammerless magnums that have been bored out to 8 bore and chambered for the standard load, and have passed the appropriate proof test.

I think that it can be generally agreed that the 8 bore loaded with 2 ounces (57 g) of no. 1 or 2 shot will kill with certainty at 70 yards (64 m), and that providing the gun weighs over 12 lbs (5.44 kg) recoil would be no more noticeable than with a magnum 12 bore. Where the use of such a gun is permitted a wildfowler armed with a double 8 bore would have the most effective goose–shooting weapon it is possible for a person of average build to use with relative ease.

10 Bore Shotgun

Compared with the 8 bore's history, the decline and rebirth of the 10 bore is far more spectacular. At the turn of this century, the European 10 bore shotgun was definitely the lightweight of the wildfowler's armoury. The average double barrel 10 bore of the time was a hammer gun weighing about $8\frac{1}{2}$ pounds (3.86 kg) with 32 inch (81 cm) barrels and throwing $1\frac{1}{2}$ ounces (71 g) of shot from its standard $2\frac{7}{8}$ inch cartridges. Such a weapon had a maximum effective range of about 60 yards (54.86 m), and was light enough to be carried for long periods by the shore gunner, a factor which certainly caused many shore based wildfowlers to choose the 10 bore rather than the much heavier double 8 or single 4 as their standard weapoon. As the 10 bore evolved the longer cartridge of $3\frac{1}{2}$ inches in Europe and Britain, so the gun became progressively heavier but still it retained its advantages of lightness compared to other wildfowling guns. Two factors then caused the 10 bore's popularity to plunge to such an extent that it very nearly went the way of the 14, 24, and 32 bores — into extinction.

The first of these factors I have already described; the inter–war depression and its effect on the prices of guns and heavy cartridges. As with the 4 and 8 bore, the use of the 10 bore as a general wildfowling gun became progressively less economic, as ammunition firms cut back their production so as to produce only the two shortest cartridge lengths of $2\frac{5}{8}$ inches and $2\frac{7}{8}$ inches. It was the second factor, however, which almost dealt the killer blow. The 12 bore was developed to accommodate a 3 inch (75 mm) cartridge which, in North American ammunition, held the same weight of shot as the standard 10 bore load. In the face of competition with the lighter, less costly 12 bore magnum with its equal shot loads in cheaper and more readily available ammunition, the 10 bore faded rapidly from the wildfowling scene in the Old World.

In North America the development of the 12 bore magnum's ballistics eventually created the situation where the smaller gun would actually out–perform the larger in terms of range, pattern and penetration. Under this sort of competition the all–American 10 bore ceased production in the 1940's. The 10 bore is, however, the largest shotgun that one can legally use in most parts of North America, so there remained a small hard core of 'big gun' users whose needs were supplied by a small import quota of single and double 10 bores made in southern Europe.

Only in the last few years have the innovations in cartridge manufacture with which the American firms led the world (plastic compression–formed cases, crimp closure and shot protecting wads) been brought into their 10 bore lines. This, together with the new 'super-magnum' $3\frac{1}{2}$ inch cartridge they introduced, has made the 10 bore once again superior to the 12 bore magnum in power and range. These super–magnum 10 bore cartridges, loaded with 2 ounces (57 g) or $2\frac{1}{4}$ ounce (66 g) of shot, can be equated to the standard 8 bore load of Britain and Europe. The 10 bore's popularity is now once more on the increase, accelerated also by the growing legislative insistence on using 'steel' shot on waterfowl haunts so as to avoid ingested lead poisoning among the fauna. In 1974 Ithaca produced what was the world's first automatic–loading big bore gun as their 'Mag 10' model. Shortly after this Marlin, and Harrington and Richardson also produced and began to market 10 bore magnum shotguns that were wholly American built.

The American 10 bore revival has had its echoes in the gun trade in Europe, as their more traditional single and double 10 bore guns are now chambered for the heavy cartridge, and sales of these guns are showing a steady increase in Britain and other European countries. Although the 10 bore seems to be growing in popularity, on both sides of the Atlantic, it is and always will remain a minority calibre as it really is a specialist weapon designed for extreme range shooting of wildfowl. It is, however, the largest calibre of shotgun in which a variety of weapons are at present being manufactured and for which cartridges are readily available.

12 Bore Shotguns

At the next step downwards in the shotgun gauges we come to the 12 bore. Without doubt this is by far the most popular shotgun calibre and it is reasonable to assume that there are more 12 bore guns in use throughout the world than all the other calibres put together. Why this particular size of gun has evolved as the maid-of-all-work in the shooting world is difficult to determine, as in terms of performance the original breech–loading 12 bore, 10 bore and 14 bore guns were hard to distinguish from each other. Certainly there was nothing which foretold that the 10 bore would evolve into a heavier wildfowling gun, the 14 bore would sink into obscurity and the 12 bore would emerge as the universal shotgun. It must be said that many of the early developments in the design of breech–loading shotguns were actually carried out on the 12 bore gun rather than on any of the other calibres and perhaps this tradition of experimentation led to the 12 bore becoming more varied and versatile. At any rate, by the end of the 19th century the 12 bore was acknowledged as the primary sporting shotgun calibre in Europe, Britain and North America and this still further increased the pace at which it was developed.

Although the original spherical ball for the gun weighed $1\frac{1}{3}$ ounces (38 g), the actual shot load for a 12 bore in the early 1900's ranged from 1–$1\frac{1}{2}$ ounces (28–35 g). Most guns at the time were built to take either the $2\frac{1}{2}$ inch (65 mm) cartridge and a maximum of $1\frac{1}{8}$ ounces (32 g) or the $2\frac{3}{4}$ inch (70 mm) case holding $1\frac{1}{4}$ ounces (35 g), but development up to the 1930's had seen the addition of, on the one hand, the ultra-lightweight 2 inch (50 mm) chambered gun taking $\frac{7}{8}$ ounce (25 g), and on the other, the 3 inch (75 mm) gun taking $1\frac{1}{2}$ ounces (42 g) or more shot. With such a wide variety of cartridge lengths and loads to choose from, the 12 bore began to take on a variety of specialised roles, depending on the load for which it was built. All the calibres larger than the 12 had one identifiable role only, that of heavy and powerful wildfowling weapons, but the 12 bore evolved a number of different types of weapon particularly suited to a certain quarry species or mode of shooting.

The standard English game gun was designed for fast handling and weighed about $6\frac{1}{4}$ pounds (2.84 kg) and, because most driven game was shot at ranges below 35 yards (32 m), was chambered for the light $2\frac{1}{2}$ (65 mm) cartridge. The British shooting public has tended to work towards the lightest possible load for any type of quarry and, consequently, these light 12 bore guns shot best with loads of $1\frac{1}{16}$ ounces (30 g) or 1 ounce (28 g). These guns were purpose built for driven game shooting and in capable hands they were highly effective weapons. The English quest for lighter guns and loads reached an extreme when the 2 inch (50 mm) chambered 12 bore was introduced in the 1930's. This gun, which even as a sidelock ejector double, only weighed around $5\frac{1}{2}$ pounds (3 kg) was designed to shoot what was a 20 bore load: $\frac{7}{8}$ ounce (25 g), from a 12 bore gun. The fact that these weapons were highly effective against driven game, such as partridge or grouse, was well demonstrated in the few years in which the 2 inch (50 mm) chambered gun rode on a wave of popularity.

Times were changing, however, and these weapons showed their major flaw in that they were limited, by their chamber length, to shooting birds at relatively close range. In the changing social structure of post-World War II Britain, more and more people were taking to 'rough shooting' and the days of the grand shooting parties were numbered. This change in the style of shooting coincided with a sharp increase in the cost of producing best English guns and imported guns from the European continent and America began to flood the market. This new style of rough shooting resembled the type of shooting most often found in Europe and North America, in that birds were walked-up and a far wider variety of quarry species were sought than was expected at a driven shoot. Birds were shot at rather longer ranges and this gave rise to the appearance of the 'general purpose' game gun which weighed from $6\frac{1}{2}$ pounds (3.45 kg) to 7 pounds (3.73 kg) and was chambered for the $2\frac{3}{4}$ inch (70 mm) cartridge and $1\frac{1}{4}$ ounces (35 g) of shot. This weapon really is an all rounder in that, irrespective of the actual design of the gun, be it single shot, repeater, or double barrel gun, a 12 bore with $2\frac{3}{4}$ (70 mm) chambers could be pressed into service and perform reasonably well in practically all kinds of shooting situations and against all quarry species.

The 3 inch (75 mm) chambered gun, which was developed in Britain and Europe, was built to shoot loads of up to $1\frac{1}{2}$ ounces (42 g) and it was this weapon which really brought about the demise of the 10 bore as a wildfowling gun. Its 12 bore replacement weighed something between $7\frac{1}{4}$ pounds (3.84 kg) and $7\frac{1}{2}$ pounds (3.96 kg), and it became known as the 'duck gun'. The North American arms' manufacturers saw the potential of this long 12 bore cartridge and they take the credit for developing the 12 bore 'magnum' gun.

I think it can generally be agreed that both European and North American shooting preferences have contrasted markedly with those of Britain, in that the two continents tend to develop progressively more power per calibre rather than lighter loads. Thus the 3 inch (75 mm) chambered North American magnum was built to take shot lods up to $1\frac{7}{8}$ ounces (53 g), barely $\frac{1}{8}$ ounce (3.5 g) less than the standard load for an 8 bore. Obviously guns have to be correspondingly heavier in order to absorb the increased recoil and many of these magnum 12 bores run to 8 pounds (3.48 kg) or over. Even so, such is the design and handling characteristics of modern guns that the 3 inch (75 mm) and $2\frac{3}{4}$ inch (70 mm) chambered 12 bores can just as easily be loaded with light game loads and will perform quite satisfactorily against upland game in North America or walked–up grouse in Britain. It is this versatility which I think has made the 12 bore the universal gun it is today, and it is likely to remain so despite the modern developments in the variety of cartridges and loads in the smaller calibres. If you were to ask a person who had never seen, let alone handled a shotgun, what shotgun calibres exist, his first words would probably be "twelve bore"; no more need be said.

16 Bore Shotgun

Since the early 1900's the 16 bore has also shown a steady decline. It was originally designed as a weapon which, though significantly lighter than a 12 bore, had a very similar range and performance. In the days of its greatest popularity the average 12 bore weighed about $6\frac{3}{4}$ pounds (3.56 kg) and the average 20 bore (which was considered a ladies' or youths' gun) weighed about $5\frac{1}{2}$ pounds (2.4 kg). At that time the 16 bore held an intermediate position between the more popular calibres, weighing around 6 pounds (2.72 kg) and firing approximately 1 ounce (28 g) loads of shot. Though it was not a weapon that was often seen on the shooting field the 16 bore, nevertheless, had a strong following among those for whom the 12 bore was just that little bit too heavy for comfortable use and the 20 bore was too light and short ranged. The calibre became identified as the 'heavy gun' for ladies or for the boy who had outgrown the 20 bore and was not ready for the 12.

The refinements made in the shotgun since the early 1900's have done much to erode the good middle position held by the 16 bore. In Britain especially, the trend towards shorter barrels which culminated in Churchill's 25 inch (63.5 cm) barrelled guns and the general improvement in the efficiency of powders led to the development of progressively lighter 12 bore guns, until the 12 bore game gun and the 16 bore were built to the same weight. The 12 bore, however, possessed the greater versatility in that it could shoot a wider variety of shot loads.

At one time the 16 bore was even held to be the most commonly used calibre in many European countries and it has been largely due to the competition from, and the market demands, of Britain and North America that the 16 bore was replaced by the more widely developed 12 bore. However, on the European continent the 16 bore still remains far more popular than it is in either Britain or North America. One factor which could explain its continuing popularity in Europe is that European manufacturers tend to produce rather heavy guns for their home market. Their double barrel and repeating 12 bore guns are usually rather heavier than their British counterparts, so that the 16 bore does to some extent retain its advantage of lightness.

As the largest of the 'small gauge' shotguns the 16 bore is generally considered unsuitable for such long range sport as wildfowling but, as with all guns, providing the quarry is within range (for the 16 bore about 45 yards (41 m)) and providing the gun is held straight it is equally as effective as a 12 bore. Weighing around the 6 pound mark (2.72 kg) and shooting a $1\frac{1}{8}$ ounce (32 g) load from its $2\frac{3}{4}$ inch (70 mm) cartridge, the 16 bore user is unlikely to find himself restricted in terms of range or killing power, yet he has a gun which can be carried all day and is easy to point and swing on to fast moving birds. This, particularly, makes the gun suitable for upland game shooting in North America or walked-up snipe shooting in Britain and Europe. Nevertheless, the development of the 20 bore over the last decade has only served to reinforce the fact that the 16 bore is very much a minority weapon and is even more likely to continue on its long slow decline. Certainly one of the symptoms of its minority status is evident in the fact that the 16 bore reloading components are far more difficult to obtain than those for either the 12 or the 20 bores and the rationalisation of many arms and ammunition manufacturers' lines in the worldwide economic recession of the late 1970's has not changed the status of the 16 bore for the better.

20 Bore Shotgun

After the 12 bore, in terms of universal popularity the 20 bore and the .410 vie with each other for second place. The 20 bore has always had a strong following of supporters ever since it evolved, in the early days of this century, as the ideal ladies' or boys' gun for driven game shooting in Britain; this is also reflected in its popularity as a youths' gun in North America. There were three main reasons for this.

The average double barrel 20 bore chambered to take the $2\frac{1}{2}$ inch (65 mm) or $2\frac{3}{4}$ inch (70 mm) cartridge weighed only about $5\frac{1}{2}$ pounds (2.4 kg), thus making it light enough to be handled easily even by small boys or lightly built ladies. In the hot summer days on the grouse moors of Britain, or in countries with warmer climates, this lightness also proved to be a blessing which made the gun popular among men. Being a smaller calibre than the 12 bore, the cartridges took up correspondingly less space, so that more could be carried in a cartridge bag — an important factor when quail shooting in North America or when shooting snipe in the tropics, where there is little opportunity of returning to base in order to replenish the supply half way through the day. The third factor is that, even though the 20 bore is a 'small gauge' weapon and fires a load of $\frac{7}{8}$ ounce (25 g) from its standard cartridge, it still remains a very effective gun for all types of shooting where the game is taken at relatively close ranges (under 35 yards or 32 m) and where a light and quick handling gun is essential.

In Britain the light double 20 bore remains the most popular type of gun in this calibre; it is in North America that two other types of 20 bore shotgun have been developed. In that continent the proud tradition of shooting sports reaches a far greater cross-section of the public and far more boys and girls learn to handle and use guns at an early age. This produced a demand for a light, simple, inexpensive 'knockabout' gun which was, nevertheless, an effective game-killing weapon with which the child could take his first steps into the world of shotgun shooting. The type of gun developed by such manufacturers as Winchester, Stevens and Ithaca were single barrel, single shot 20 bores with 'drop down' opening (much like a conventional double gun), shortened stock with fitted recoil pad and a shorter than average, open bored barrel. Although this format has now been copied by many European manufacturers, in order to compete in the American market, this is a characteristic American design and it performs its task admirably.

As described earlier in this chapter, the American arms manufacturers, in answer to the demands of their home market, have tended to develop any particular gauge of gun to shoot progressively heavier loads in order to gain greater versatility in any gun's performance. The 20 bore, already a popular calibre, was developed on the heels of the 12 bore, so that at the present time a suitably chambered 20 bore can handle any shot load up to $1\frac{1}{4}$ ounces (35 g); that is, the equivalent of a medium 12 bore cartridge. The increasing shot load has, however, meant that these 'magnum' 20 bore guns have to be built at a correspondingly greater weight. The effect of this is that these 20 bores tend to be too heavy for ladies or learners, but appeal to sportsmen who require the ability to shoot a wide range of loads from a gun of small calibre. Even 20 bore magnum cartridges still take up less space than 12 bore cases, so some of the initial appeal of the 20 bore as a calibre has not been lost and the increased variety of potential loads for the gun has certainly added to the attraction of this gauge of gun. Certainly very many sportsmen (like myself), who first started shooting with a 20 bore gun will testify to the effectiveness of the calibre against all manner of game in a wide variety of conditions. Like so many things we derived great enjoyment from when we were children, the 20 bore will always be looked upon with affection, and the sheer joy of using this calibre, as experienced by many of its followers must surely stem from these roots.

28 Bore Shotgun

Of all the shotgun calibres in regular use, the 28 bore must be the rarest. In North America it suffers by falling between two well developed and popular gauges — the 20 and the .410, and in Britain it competes with the 4 bore as the least used shotgun. From my own observations I feel that there are more 8 bores on active service in Britain than there are 28 bores but even so, there is currently a slowly growing movement on both sides of the Atlantic for this little weapon.

The shot load for the 28 bore varies from $\frac{5}{8}$ ounce (18 g) to $\frac{3}{4}$ ounce (21 g) depending on whether a $2\frac{1}{2}$ inch (65 mm) or a $2\frac{3}{4}$ inch (70 mm) cartridge is used.

This load is quite effective against most species of game provided shots are taken at distances of around 30 yards (27.43 m). Because of this, and because of the history of the .410 calibre, the 28 bore is generally considered in Europe and Britain to be the smallest 'serious' game gun. Due to its light load and limited range, however, its use has to be restricted to close range work in thick cover, such as woodcock shooting or other close range sports, such as decoying woodpigeon or walked-up rabbit shooting.

Compared to its larger cousin, the 20 bore, there has been very little development of the 20 bore cartridge so that no heavy or magnum loads are available. This lack of variety certainly leads the American shotgunner to consider the 28 bore as an upland gun only, not suitable for wildfowl shooting except in very special circumstances. When considered as a quail gun in skilled hands the gauge can be very effective indeed, but the 28 bore is, nevertheless, far less versatile than either the 20 or the .410 bore. As a child's first shotgun I consider the 28 bore to be ideal, as an average double gun in the calibre weighs around 5 to 5½ pounds (2.3–2.4 kg) which is light enough to allow even the smallest nine year old to swing with ease. Its rather restricted shot load means that, although the gun is less versatile, the gun's weight is matched to the cartridge and recoil does not present the problem it does in a light .410 using 3 inch (75 mm) cartridges. Similarly, the light load teaches the child to be selective with his choice of shots and stresses the need to let the game come into the gun's range.

Unfortunately though, many manufacturers overlook this calibre when they produce guns for youngsters, preferring to produce 20 and .410 guns instead, and these two calibres with their wide variety of loads and consequent versatility of uses, have swept the 28 bore into a minority position. Although, as I stated earlier, there are now indications that the 28 bore may be gaining slowly in the popularity stakes and may even become more popular than it ever has been, it will never seriously compete with either the 20 or the .410 until a wider variety of loads are developed for the calibre and many more arms manufacturers start producing and marketing the 28 bore in quantity.

.410 Gauge Shotgun

The last and smallest of the centre-fire shotgun calibres, the .410 gauge, started from very modest and lowly beginnings. The original cartridge length was 2 inches (50 mm) and this held a maximum of ³⁄₈ ounce (10.6 g) of shot. The gun was originally designed for such purposes as rat-shooting around farmyards, where the use of a rifle or other shotgun calibre would endanger other farm animals, buildings and people. As a close range 'rat gun' it proved to be very effective and many .410 users derived great pleasure from using such a light and handy weapon. Thus the demand for a longer and more powerful cartridge arose out of the wishes of many .410 users to extend into other areas of pest control, such as woodpigeon or crow shooting and the 2½ inch (65 mm) cartridge was developed. This greater case length allowed the cartridge to be loaded with ½ ounce (14 g) of shot and the weapon became quite useful for short range pest and even game shooting. In the more traditional British game shooting scene even this increased load was still considered as rather too light for effective use against game and the .410 is not even now regarded as a 'proper' game gun. This is a great pity, as I have one shooting friend who takes great toll of driven partridge using a bolt action repeating .410 and 2½ inch (65 mm) cartridges.

It was soon realised that this calibre could be bored out to take a 3 inch (75 mm) cartridge case and these extra length cartridges added a great deal of extra power and versatility to the weapon. With one .410 shotgun it was possible, using the shortest cartridge, to shoot rats in enclosed barns or other large farm buildings and, with the 3 inch (75 mm) cartridges shoot game at the normal shooting distances of up to 35 yards (32 m). The 3 inch (75 mm) case held a maximum load of ¾ ounce (21 g), and it was this heavy load and the increased overall versatility it brought to the calibre which caused the .410 to eclipse the 28 bore as a popular lightweight shotgun for the very young beginner or as a 'fun gun' for pest control and other informal shooting.

Only in recent years has the popularity of the .410 suffered a setback as the cost of the 3 inch (75 mm) cartridge has soared in comparison with that of the standard 28 bore loaded cartridges. Added to this fact is the realisation that the narrower the bore diameter of any given weapon, the less efficiently it will shoot a given load. Therefore the 28 bore 2¾ inch (70 mm) chambered gun will throw far better patterns than the same shot load from a .410 bore, all other things being equal; it is these two facts which have recently caused the revival of interest in the 28 bore. Nevertheless, the .410 ranks equal to the 20 bore as one of the more universally known of shotgun calibres and the scale of production by virtually all the arms

Figure 2.3   Comparison of cartridges to show bore sizes. *Left to right* — .410, 28, 20, 16, 12, 10 (*standard*), 10 (*Magnum*), 8, 4

manufacturers in Europe and North America is likely to keep the .410 at this status in the future.

.360 (9 mm) Bore Shotgun

The only other remaining shotgun I will mention very briefly is the .360 or 9 mm gun. This fires the Flobert type rimfire paper or brass cartridge and the gauge is often referred to as the 'garden gun'. Indeed with a shot load of $\frac{3}{16}$ ounce (5 g) the only effective role such a light weapon can fulfil is to control birds in gardens or orchards, where larger calibres stand the risk of damaging fruit or plants. I do not think that anybody could consider the calibre as suitable for any other purpose except, perhaps, for fun shooting at thrown tin cans or for gun safety training.

This then is the variety of bores or calibres that are currently in use in parts of Britain, Europe and North America. Each calibre was originally designed to serve one type of shooting, but as time has gone by many of these original bores have diminished in availability and popularity while others have been developed to fulfil a multitude of roles. Nowadays, with the great versatility that has been evolved in such calibres as the 12, 20 and .410 gauges the choice of weapon for a great many shooting situations lies far more with the shooter's personal preference than it has ever done before.

LOCK, STOCK AND BARREL

Most sports or pastimes which generate their own specialised vocabulary tend to produce one or two terms that 'escape' and become adopted into general usage in the language. A good example of this is the now universally used phrase 'lock, stock and barrel' which originally described the three essentials of any shoulder firearm. The lock was the mechanism by which the loaded charge was ignited, the stock was the device for resting the weapon against the shoulder, and the barrel was the tube through which the projectile or projectiles were launched by the burning gases behind them when the gun was fired. From the days of the earlier, shoulder held firearms to the weapons of the present day these three essentials have remained unchanged, in that without any of them the weapon in question will not function correctly, if at all. What has changed, of course, is the complexity and variety of each of these three components, and each time some new design or variation is introduced it tends to generate new specialist terms.

The Lock

Of the three components, it is the lock which has undergone the greatest change and diversification through the shotgun's evolution from the days of the flintlock to the present. This diversification I will deal with in greater detail when I describe the main types of shotgun in the next three chapters, but for the present, a very brief description will be enough. Nowadays the 'locks' of a gun generally refer to the more traditional designs of shotgun such as double-barrel, side-by-side or over-and-under. In this kind of weapon there are two main styles of lock. The side-lock, in which the mechanism which cocks and releases the hammers (or tumblers) is positioned on the side of the weapon, and the box-lock — also called the 'Anson and Deely' action after its inventors — in which the mechanisms are placed under and behind the breech of the gun. On all other types of gun the word lock has been replaced by 'action'; therefore 'bolt action' describes a firing mechanism within a sliding bolt, 'pump action' denotes a mechanism which is cocked by a 'pumping movement' of a sliding forearm, and a 'lever action' is one where the mechanism is worked by a lever behind the trigger.

The Stock

A stock, nowadays, can be made in a great variety of styles which have been developed over the years to suit a particular method of shooting. There are, however, only three main styles of shotgun stock in common use, and the other variations tend to be adaptations of one of these three to suit a particular purpose.

Undoubtedly the original style of stock had a straight hand grip, and this is known as the 'straight' or 'English' stock: the purpose of this straight grip was to allow the trigger hand to move backwards slightly when firing the second barrel of a double gun. It was claimed that this made the movement of the trigger finger from the front to the back trigger that much quicker; whether or not this is the case is open to debate. However, this style of stock is still very popular in Britain and other countries where the double side-by-side is the most commonly used form of shotgun.

When repeating and automatic loading shotguns were developed, many shooters found shooting more comfortable if the hand of the stock is shaped into a 'pistol grip'. This type of grip allows the hand to take a firmer and more positive grip so that there was less danger of the hand slipping backwards during the gun's recoil. Nowadays the 'pistol grip' stock is definitely the most popular style, universally, and it is also used on single trigger, double-barrel guns and on single shot weapons. The most common variation on the pistol grip stock is the 'Monte Carlo' stock, which has a raised comb and cheek-piece. This style, which probably gets its name from the live pigeon competitions held in Monte Carlo in years gone by, tends to make the gun shoot high of the aiming point and is popular where rising targets are shot at, for instance in Olympic Trap clay pigeon shooting.

The third type of stock which is occasionally seen is the 'swan neck' style, which is something between the first two. The hand of the stock is more steeply angled than it is on a straight stock, but it does not have the cut-away appearance of a pistol grip stock, so it is considered by many to be more elegant than either of the other two main styles.

Arguments will probably continue to rage as to which style is best, but it really comes down to personal preference and comfort. A person will always shoot his best with the weapon which is most comfortable for him to hold, and whether this has a straight, pistol, or swan neck grip is strictly a personal factor.

The Barrel

The construction methods employed in barrel making varies amongst arms manufacturers and each style of shotgun. Each maker has his own pet method of producing gun barrels which is claimed to be better, for one reason or another, than his rivals; the end result, however, of each of these individual processes is a tube of a given internal bore diameter which is reamed out to slightly over–size at one end to receive the cartridge, and has a varied amount of constriction at the other end depending on the degree and type of choke boring.

At one time chamberless guns were made, but the tendency of the burning gases to blow round the wads gave rather poor velocity and penetration. This was improved by boring out the breech end of the gun to accommodate the cartridge and this area was known as the gun's chamber. The difference in the true bore diameter and the diameter of the chamber is made to correspond to the thickness of the cartridge case, so that the wadding in the cartridge case forms a gas seal in the barrel when the cartridge is fired. The length of cartridge that any barrel could accept used to depend on the length of the over–size portion on the breech end of the barrel; therefore a 12 bore gun chambered for a 2½ inch (65 mm) case could not accept a 3 inch (75 mm) long case because the latter is actually longer than the reamed out chamber in the barrel.

More efficient use of the internal space of the cartridge by means of more compact and plastic wads in recent years has meant, however, that this rule is not now as rigid as it once was and it is possible to purchase cartridges loaded with 3

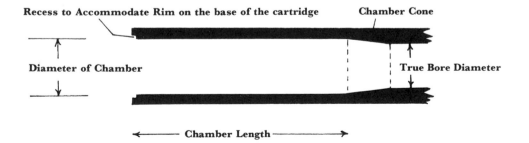

Figure 2.4   Cross section of a shotgun's chamber

inch (75 mm) loads and generating high 'magnum' pressures when they are fired, which will fit into a shorter chambered gun. This, of course, is very dangerous and we must always choose cartridges that are designated as suitable for the shotgun we use regardless of the actual length of the cartridge case. It must also be remembered that the chamber is bored to take the fired case, so an unfired cartridge of greater length can often fit into the chamber.

At the breech end of the chamber a groove or step is cut to accommodate the rim of the cartridge and at the other end the barrel wall tapers down to the true bore diameter of the gun and this taper is known as the 'chamber cone'. The length of the cone averages about $\frac{1}{2}$ inch (13 mm) but some gunmakers in the past have experimented with both shorter and longer cones only to come to the conclusion that the length of cone has little effect on the charge's velocity providing the wadding column within the cartridge is longer than the cone and the correct cartridge case length for the gun's chamber is used. Here the 3 inch (75 mm) chambered .410 shotgun is seen as a disadvantage as, when using $2\frac{1}{2}$ inch (65 mm) or 2 inch (50 mm) cases, burning gases can actually blow past the wads before they form an efficient seal at the end of the chamber cone. This lack of an efficient gas seal (or obturation as it is called) produces a poorer performance.

The true barrel starts at the end of the chamber cone and this should have a uniform bore diameter until it reaches the muzzle-end, if the barrel is not choked in any way. This un-choked or 'true cylinder' barrel is nowadays used only on close range game guns or on guns specifically designed to shoot single ball or slug loads. In most other guns, the last 4 inches (10 cm) or so before the muzzle are altered in some way in order to vary the spread of shot at any given distance.

The Choke

Before going on to describe the four ways in which a choke section of a barrel can be constructed, some knowledge of what a choke is designed to do is needed. For most shotguns the distance of 40 yards (36.6 m) is taken as the standard at which patterns of shot are tested and compared, and a 30 inch (76 cm) circle is taken as the standard diameter of spread analysis. At this range, providing the barrel is correctly bored, a true cylinder of any gauge will throw forty per cent of the shot charge into a 30 inch circle. Here let me state that there is a commonly held belief that narrower bores throw narrower patterns and larger bores throw wider spreads of shot: this is totally incorrect. All other things being equal the 4 bore and .410 will both throw the same spread at a given range.

The lightest degree of choke, improved cylinder is designed to increase this percentage to fifty and this is often confused with one-quarter choke which should throw fifty-five per cent. Half choke (also known as modified choke) should put sixty per cent of the shot charge into the circle and this is increased to sixty-five per cent in three-quarter, or improved modified choke, and seventy per cent in full choke. The whole idea of choke boring is to hold the shot charge together, thereby restricting the spread so that game can be shot at greater distances than would be possible with a cylinder bored gun. Thus a well bored full choke barrel will throw the same spread of shot at 55 yards (50.3 m), forty per cent shot in 30 inch (76 cm) circle, as a true cylinder barrel will at 40 yards (36.6 m). It is therefore only natural that birds, such as wildfowl, which are shot at relatively greater distances (from 40 to 50 yards (36.6-45.7 m) with an average 12 bore)call for a gun with tightly choked barrels. Duck guns or wildfowling magnums usually have full choke barrels as a result of the demand for long range killing shot patterns.

At the other end of the scale, guns which are used for close range work, for instance driven partridge in Europe or walked-up quail in North America need to be open bored so that the shot pattern can spread quickly. A bird killed at close range with a heavily choked gun often takes so much shot that it is unfit for eating. Skeet shooting, the close range clay pigeon shooting discipline, demands a very rapid spread of shot indeed as the targets are often taken at ranges of less than 15 yards (13.7 m); how the manufacturers have set about trying to achieve this will be described later, along with the different methods of choking a gun.

As well as making the gun unsuitable for close range shooting heavy choking can also cause pattern qualities to deteriorate and this has led many sportsmen to have their guns bored more open. As the shot travels up the barrel in the instant after the trigger of the gun has been pulled, it is inevitable that some of the shot will be in contact with the barrel wall and these will become deformed and a few may not even reach the target at 40 yards (36.6 m)! In a heavily choked gun the number of deformed pellets per charge is greatly increased because the shot is squashed together to an even greater degree as it passes through the choke section. This final squashing of the shot charge may cause the gun to throw uneven patterns with pellets grouped together and large empty spaces within the 30 inch (76 cm) circle.

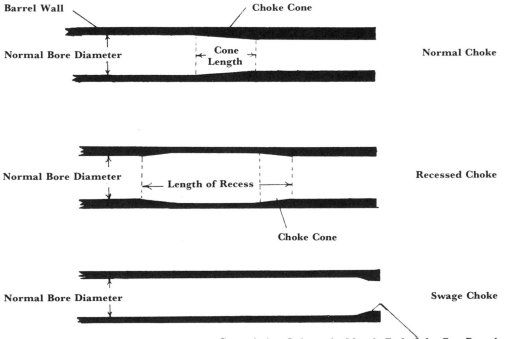

Figure 2.5   Types of chokes

Recent advances in cartridge design, in particular the use of the one piece, shot protecting, cup type wad has, to a great extent, eliminated this crushing. Even so, a pellet count from two identical cartridges, one fired through a cylinder barrel and the other through a full choke barrel would usually give a higher number of shot on target for the cylinder.

It is still true, however, that even with these new shot protecting wads it is inevitable that some shot will be crushed, deformed, and lost to the pattern by its passage through the choke section. In a similar way, it is a general principle that the narrower the bore, the greater is the proportion of shot in contact with the barrel wall when the shot travels up the barrel. Therefore, even though a $3\frac{1}{2}$ inch (9 cm) 10 bore can fire the same load as a standard 8 bore, the smaller gun's pattern tends to be inferior because of the barrel–wall deformation of the shot.

Methods of Choking

There are four main methods by which a shotgun barrel is choked. Three of these are designed to concentrate the shot pattern to the different standards I have specified from improved cylinder to full choke, and one method is designed to accelerate the dispersal of the shot.

'Normal choke' is built by reducing the barrel diameter to the required degree in a gentle cone shape, and this occurs between 2 and 4 inches (5 and 10 cm) from the muzzle. From the end of the choke cone to the muzzle the tube is again parallel. Most guns are choked in this way, and this method of choking has the great advantage that it is the easiest to alter. For instance it is a simple matter for a gunmaker to open out the boring from full to half choke by a bit of careful enlargement of the choke cone.

In recent years a number of European arms manufacturers have turned to 'swage' choking whereby only the last $\frac{1}{2}$ inch (13 mm) before the muzzle is constricted. This has the advantage that it is a simple operation, often done by machine, and it therefore adds less to the cost of a gun than carefully bored 'normal' choke. In terms of performance there is little to choose between the two methods, but they both suffer from one major disadvantage; in both cases it is a simple operation to remove the choke, that is to open out the bore and, therefore, the pattern but choke cannot be added again once it has been removed.

In order to do this the third choking method has to be employed, although this is not nearly as effective as the first two. To increase the amount of constriction near the gun's muzzle, the bore is enlarged just before the choke cone starts. This increases the amount of relative constriction between the large bore diameter and the minimum diameter of the choke cone and has the effect of increasing the amount of choke; thereby decreasing the spread of shot. This choking method is known as 'recessed' choke and is not considered to be as successful in terms of the regularity and evenness of the shot spread as either normal or swage choke.

The last choking method is rather the reverse of the other three. In some shooting disciplines even a true cylinder barrel throws patterns that are too dense, so some method of increasing the shot spread is used. The most common of these is known as 'reverse' choke or retro choke in which the bore is progressively enlarged near the muzzle to give a slight 'bell mouth'. In practise this allows the shot to start spreading fractionally before it leaves the gun's muzzle and quite effectively increases the spread of the pattern. This type of choking is most often found in shotguns built for shooting in skeet clay pigeon shooting events.

Variable Choke Devices

While on the subject of choke, mention must be made of the different types of variable choke devices that are currently on the market. In order to increase the versatility of single barrel guns, two systems for varying the choke have evolved.

The first of these is the 'replaceable choke tube' system, by which tubes of different constriction and therefore choke are either screwed onto the end of the barrel, or sunk into the muzzle. When a different choke is required, one choke tube is removed and the replacement is fitted in its place. While this can be time consuming, the bore of the choke attachments can be very accurately made so as to throw consistently accurate patterns for the degree of choke, and the choke tubes can be designed so as not to interfere to any great extent with the gun's handling properties.

By way of contrast, the 'variable' choke attachment works on a sort of diaphragm principle whereby the bore diameter inside the device can be altered by turning the choke control ring. While this is both a quick and convenient method of changing the choke, these devices are often heavy and tend to throw rather less consistent patterns than the choke tubes. Their weight detracts from the gun's balance and their bulky appearance on the end of the barrel does nothing, in my opinion, for the gun's looks. They do remain, however, the easiest method of altering the choke on a single barrel gun and this may outweigh their other disadvantages.

The Cartridge

The cartridge has only five basic components in that it consists of the case, primer or cap, powder, wadding, and shot, but each of these can be varied in order to produce ammunition for specific purposes. While the design of the shotgun has remained static, apart from minor innovations, since the early 1900's, the shotgun cartridge has been developed to a far greater extent, with a great deal of innovation and modification coming in the last twenty years or so.

At one time practically all cartridges had 'paper' cases which were cut from a roll of suitably glued and impregnated paper. The base of this tube was fitted with the brass cartridge head and the joint was reinforced by a compressed paper internal base wad. While this was an efficient and simple design, paper cases had one major disadvantage in that they were prone to swell (when they got damp) to such an extent that they became unusable. Since the 1950's therefore, the use of plastic instead of paper has, for the first time, made shotgun ammunition really waterproof.

It has also given rise to two different kinds of cartridge case which are known as 'parallel tube' and 'compression formed' cases. The former is made in the same way as the paper case but the latter is formed as a one piece moulding. The compression formed case, an American idea, is in many ways the better of the two in that it allows for a more efficient combustion of the powder charge and it has a higher resistance to cracking and warping than the parallel tube case. Recently there has been a great revival in the hobby of cartridge reloading and for this purpose the compression formed cartridge case is far more durable than the tube case, in some instances being capable of being re-used up to ten or fifteen times.

The primer or cap, seated in the centre of the base of the cartridge, provides the ignition system. At one time a mercuric compound based on Forsyth's fulminate was used in the primer, but it suffered from two disadvantages. Firstly, it was sensitive to extremes of temperature and this affected its ignition properties and, secondly, the residue from the flame was highly corrosive. Gun barrels which were not carefully cleaned after use very soon showed signs of corrosion. Nowadays, very few cartridge manufacturers use a mercuric compound and it has been superceded by a variety of far more efficient and stable fulminates which are also non-corrosive.

A wide variety of powders are used in shotgun cartridges and these are designed so that variation in the rate of burning and consequent pressure and velocity are possible. All modern powders are based on a 'nitro' compound and are generally termed 'low bulk' powders, that is, they take up far less volume than the old black powder. They do, however, generate far higher pressures and cannot be safely used in guns which were designed and proved for black powder only. In Britain and many other European countries there are legal restrictions on the sale of guns that are not 'nitro proved' and to my knowledge no breach loading guns are made that are not submitted to nitro proof of some sort.

Wadding

Plastic and nylon are now widely used as wadding material and it is this that has brought about great improvements in shotgun ballistics in recent years. The purpose of the wadding in a cartridge is to seal the exploding gases so that as much energy as possible is used to push the shot load out of the barrel. Its piston-like action not only seals the gases but also drives the shot charge before it. Up until quite recently the wads were made of either felt or cork which were topped with thin card, but to a great extent this has been superceded by the 'all-in-one' plastic wad. Not only does this perform the same task as the felt or cork wads, but it also protects the shot from barrel deformation by means of a thin, forward pointing shot cup. This has a significant effect on the spread and quality of the pattern. Although there are arguments against the use of plastic wads, on the grounds of conservation — wads can easily be accidentally eaten by cattle or wild animals — plastic wads are now far more widely used than any of the older materials.

Shot

Shot comes in a wide variety of sizes. These range from the 'spherical ball' (which is one per cartridge) and rifled slug, both of which are used for shooting big

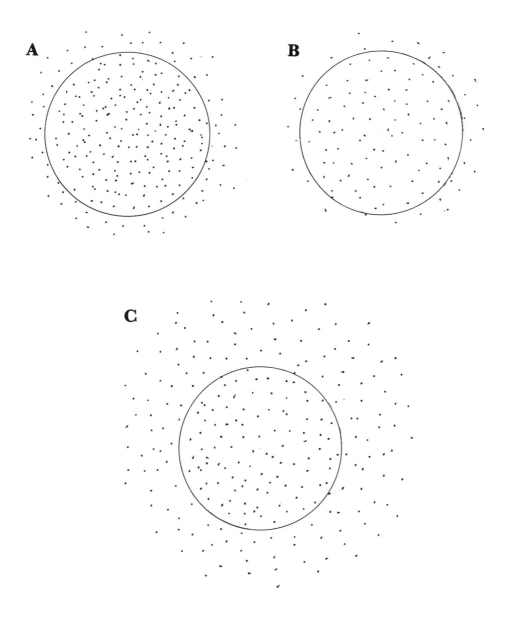

Figure 2.6   Comparison of shot patterns:
A. 12 bore 1⅛ oz no. 5 (English) full choke — 70% in 30″ circle at 40 yards (approx 172 pellets)
B. .410 bore ½ oz no. 5 (English) full choke — 70% in 30″ circle at 40 yards (approx 77 pellets)
C. 12 bore 1⅛ oz no. 5 (English) open cylinder — 40% in 30″ circle at 40 yards (approx 98 pellets)

SHOT SIZES		APPROXIMATE NUMBER OF PELLETS PER CHARGE								
U.S.	English	$1\frac{1}{2}$oz	$1\frac{1}{4}$oz	$1\frac{1}{8}$oz	1oz	$\frac{7}{8}$oz	$\frac{3}{4}$oz	$\frac{5}{8}$oz	$\frac{1}{2}$oz	$\frac{3}{8}$oz
2	1	150	125	112	100	87	75	62	50	37
4	3	210	175	157	140	122	105	87	70	52
5	4	255	212	191	170	148	125	106	85	63
6	5	330	275	247	220	192	165	137	110	82
–	6	405	337	303	270	236	202	168	135	101
$7\frac{1}{2}$	7	510	425	382	340	297	255	212	170	127
8	8	675	562	506	450	393	337	281	225	161
9	9	870	725	652	580	507	435	362	290	217

Figure 2.7   Charge Table

game, to No. 9 shot which is used for very close range shooting of small targets such as mini–clays or skeet, and averages 580 pellets to the ounce (28 g). There are some general principles which can, however, be applied to shot so that the correct size can be chosen for any particular style of shooting. What can confuse the issue in these days, when imported ammunition is sold in competition with the home produced variety is that many countries use a different numbering order of shot sizes so a comparison of shot sizes between say, American and Belgian ammunition is difficult. For simplicity, therefore, I will refer only to English and American shot sizes.

Smaller shot will increase the density of a pattern because more individual pellets are held in a given shot charge. Therefore, the actual shot count in a 30 inch (76 cm) circle from number eight shot will be much higher than an identical cartridge loaded with number four or five shot. In order to ensure that small targets such as snipe or woodcock receive sufficient hits to kill them small shot, such as number eight should be used because if larger shot is used the bird stands a much better chance of actually flying through the centre of the pattern without being struck. The disadvantage of small shot is that the lighter and smaller each individual pellet, the more rapidly does it lose its velocity and killing power (known as its 'striking energy'). A large bird such as a goose is unlikely to be killed at 55 yards (50.3 m) — the approximate maximum range for 12 bore — if it receives a charge of small shot, because much of the pellet's already decreasing energy will be expended on penetrating the dense plumage and the bird will only be wounded.

In order to ensure that larger and stronger birds, such as wildfowl, are killed cleanly at maximum range, larger sizes of shot must be used; this in turn, however, leads to fewer pellets per charge and less dense patterns. To compensate for this, heavier loads were developed and this culminated in the 'magnum' wildfowling loads which are usually only supplied in the larger sizes of shot. Even so the quality of the pattern deteriorates far sooner than the individual pellet energy of a large shot, so that tales of birds killed at distances of over 70 yards (64 m) are usually attributable to one pellet striking a vital organ rather than a good pattern. Such shots are often considered lucky but they are extremely unsporting, in that at ranges over the accepted maximum for any given load the proportion of birds wounded is far greater than those killed and many birds would suffer unnecessarily.

The largest sizes of shot, known as 'lettered shot' in Britain or 'buckshot' in America are more often used against large ground game such as wild boar in Europe or white–tailed deer in North America. Depending on the size, pellet count to the ounce varies from 8 (S.G. or 00 Buck) to 70 (B.B. or Air Rifle). With so few pellets per charge, deformation of the shot as they pass through the choke portion of a barrel can be a critical factor in the killing quality of the shot pattern, so guns made specifically for buckshot loads tend to be open bored.

Most shot is made from 'hardened' lead which contains small quantities of other ingredients, such as arsenic, in order to make the metal less prone to deformation and crushing. Since the early 19th century it has been made on the 'drop shot' principle whereby the molten lead is poured through a grid. On falling through the grid the liquid lead separates into droplets of 'lead rain' and falls some distance into a tank of cold water. In its descent the surface tension on the liquid lead droplet forms it into a perfect sphere which is immediately chilled and solidified on reaching the cold water. The length of the drop varies but, generally, the further the lead falls before reaching the cooling tank the better is the shot that is formed, so most shot is produced in 'shot towers'. After chilling, the shot is graded and sorted and any malformed lead is remelted for a further drop.

In many prime wildfowling areas of North America there has been growing concern that spent lead shot is being ingested as grit by many species of waterfowl and this leads to the birds' eventual death from slow lead poisoning. Resulting from this concern, legislation banning the use of lead shot has been put into force in many areas and a substitute has been found by using soft iron shot instead. The disadvantages of this new material, which is called 'steel shot', is that it is lighter and therefore loses its striking energy more rapidly than lead shot of the same size; there is also a risk of damaging the internal bores of the gun by using steel shot. In order to counteract the more rapid loss of velocity, larger shot is used but this means fewer shot per cartridge. This is one reason why the 10 bore is, once again, gaining in popularity as its cartridge has the necessary volume to accommodate heavy loads of steel shot.

This then has been a breakdown of the different shotgun calibres, the different chokes and the variations possible in cartridge loads that will provide some background for the succeeding chapters on the shotgun types and the variety of shooting available. The meanings of many specialist terms I have omitted from this chapter will, I hope, become apparent as you read on, but by now you should have enough of a background vocabulary to understand much of the technical jargon associated with shotgun shooting. As with any sport or pastime, to be able to speak the same language as another enthusiast is half the fun.

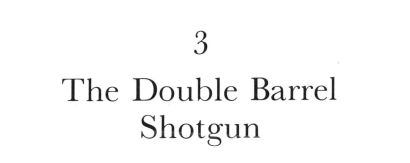

3
The Double Barrel Shotgun

Figure 3.0   Churchill 'Premiere' Sidelock (Assisted Opening)

Courtesy: Churchill Ltd

The Double Barrel Shotgun

To anybody wishing to purchase a shotgun, perhaps for the first time, or maybe to add another weapon to an already large collection, the choice of gun can be difficult. There is such a wide selection of bores, types and makes to choose from that selecting the right gun for your purpose can pose quite a problem. What I intend to do, therefore, in this and the next two chapters, is to provide a description of the main types of weapon that are currently available, in order that the reader can make up his or her own mind as to which type of gun to choose.

The shotgun with two barrels, however they may be aligned, is the most universally popular in use today. Even in North America, that stronghold of the single barrel repeating shotgun, there are probably more double barrel shotguns in use than repeaters, although this may not have been the case before World War II. The main reasons for this increase in the popularity of the double gun will be explained later in this chapter; many are built into the very design of the weapon.

Advantages of Two Barrels

Firstly, the fact that the shooter is equipped with a gun that can fire two shots at one loading certainly gave the early 19th century sportsman a decided advantage over the user of a single shot weapon. When a choice of two chokes was added later this increased the variety of shots that could be taken, because the open bored barrel could be used for close range shots and the more heavily choked barrel used for more distant opportunities. This instant choice of choke is one major advantage of a double barrel gun that cannot be incorporated into shotguns of any other design. In addition, an even wider variation is possible if cartridges containing different loads are chambered in the barrels. It is possible to choose cartridges that are designed to deal with totally different types of game. A good example of this versatility was demonstrated by a double shot, or 'right and left' as it is called, taken by my mother when shooting in India. Armed with her double 20 bore loaded with a rifled slug in one barrel and a standard load of No. 6 shot in the other, she killed a spotted deer with her first shot, and without taking the gun from her shoulder, killed a Kalege pheasant with the other. Such versatility cannot be approached using other types of shotgun. In many shooting situations of course, the shooter cannot possibly arm himself for every eventuality, but he can certainly be better prepared than a shooter using a single barrel gun.

Disadvantages

The double barrel shotgun does have a number of disadvantages inherent in its design which tends to make it unsuitable, or at least not the ideal choice of weapon, for certain situations or circumstances. The double gun's complexity, even in its simplest boxlock non-ejector form, led the North American gun industry away from this traditional design and resulted in the advent of the single barrel repeater guns which were simpler to build, assemble and maintain. The complex internal mechanism of the double gun is one which requires more craftsman hours to make than any other style of shotgun, and this meant that the better guns tend to be expensive, certainly compared with the simpler machine-made repeaters.

In addition, side-by-side shotguns in particular are usually lighter than other comparable shotgun types, and while this makes for a faster and easier handling weapon, it also produces a noticeable increase in recoil. In situations where many cartridges are used in the course of the day, as in clay pigeon shooting, the side-by-side user will be far more badly punished by recoil than users of other types of gun, and very few side-by-side guns are seen in the important national or international clay pigeon tournaments.

TYPES OF DOUBLE BARREL GUNS

Despite these disadvantages however, the traditional shotgun with two barrels still remains the most popular and widely used weapon. If I can discount the small minority of 'odd' weapons that have appeared over the years and are still made in very small numbers — the three and four barrel shotguns that have occasionally been made and the German 'Drilling' combination shotgun and rifles — the double gun comes either as a **side-by-side** or an **over-and-under**. These terms of course are self explanatory and refer to the way the barrels are arranged. The original two-barrel gun, in the early days of the flintlock, was built as an over-and-under, but near the end of the flintlock's reign gunmakers devised a method of joining barrels side-by-side and it totally superseded the over-and-under as the 'sporting gun' was developed.

Early in the 20th century, the problems which hindered the development of the breech-loading over-and-under had been finally overcome. The early attempts to revive the design had failed because it was difficult to produce a strong barrels-to-action joint without making the action very deep and ungainly, but by 1910, Boss, one of England's premier gunmakers, was marketing an over-and-under which was as elegant as the conventional side-by-side. These guns, however, were very expensive and it was only when John M. Browning's over-and-under design was first marketed in 1926 that this type of weapon became available to a far greater number of sportsmen, through being considerably cheaper than the English guns of this type produced before this date.

The Side-by-Side

For some reason the way the barrels of a double gun have been aligned seems to have caused the two types of gun to evolve in rather different ways. Of the two, the over-and-under is considered to be a far more versatile design, but whether this is true in practice is open to debate. The side-by-side shotgun is definitely considered by most shotgun users as a gun to be used mainly for shooting live birds rather than clay targets. This type of shotgun therefore has developed specialist guns to cope with the variety of winged game and has not been particularly influenced by the demands of the various clay pigeon shooting disciplines. Thus on one end of the scale there are the lightweight open-bored and short barrelled game guns, designed for fast handling and shooting of driven birds or close range work against walked-up woodcock or quail, and at the other extreme there are the heavy, long barrelled and tightly choked magnum wildfowling guns.

The styling evolved by each of these weapons makes them immediately recognisable, as each type is now made to a generally accepted successful pattern. The European and British game gun has barrels about 26 or 28 inches (66 or 71 cm) in length which are open bored, with a standard or splinter fore-end and a straight hand stock. The sighting rib between the barrels is usually either concave or flat and file cut. The wildfowling magnum side-by-side, on the other hand, usually has a 'beaver tail' fore-end full pistol grip stock and rubber recoil pad. Barrels average 30 inches (76 cm) long and are usually bored both full choke. These descriptions, however, refer to European guns, as the more general use of beaver-tail fore-ends, recoil pads and pistol grip stocks in North America serves to make this sort of identification more difficult. In fact there is a very definite difference in the styling between the average European side-by-side and its American counterpart.

Falling between the game gun and the wildfowling magnum is the general purpose side-by-side which is often referred to as a 'field' type shotgun. This kind of weapon, which, as its description implies, can be used for most bird shooting situations, usually has barrels of 28 inches (71 cm) and is most often bored full and half (modified) choke. The shape of the fore-end and stock depends on the market for which the gun is built, but the weight averages between $6\frac{1}{2}$ and 7 pounds (3–3.2 kg). This makes the gun about 1 pound (454 g) lighter than the magnum and about 8 ounces (227 g) heavier than the light game gun.

The Over-and-Under

Shotgun shooters tend to be traditionalists and conservative in their choice of weapons, so the long British and European traditions of manufacturing side-by-side sporting guns has probably been a significant factor in maintaining these regions as the side-by-side's stronghold. It is very definitely the main sporting gun of Northern and Western Europe and Britain. The over-and-under, on the other hand, has a much wider general popularity. While this style of gun is not often seen on the game shoots of Britain, it is the most common weapon among the

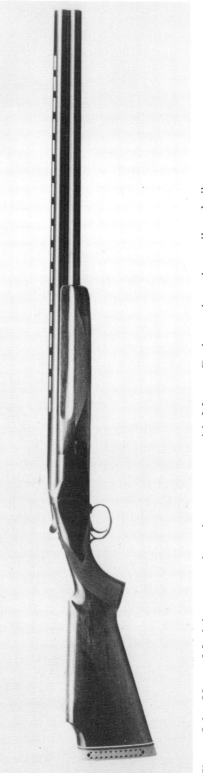

Figure 3.1   Xpert Model over-and-under trap gun with Monte Carlo stock and ventilated rib
Courtesy: Winchester Ltd

clay pigeon shooting circles throughout the world, and in North America it also competes on very favourable terms with the repeaters as the favourite bird shooting gun. Why is it then that this style of gun with its superimposed barrels has become so much more popular than its side–by–side cousin? There are a number of reasons which probably stem both from the gun's design and its history.

With one barrel placed above the other, the shooter, when the gun is mounted at his shoulder, looks along the top of one barrel only. When, as is normally the case, some sort of rib is laid along the top of this barrel, sighting or pointing the gun is considered by many shooters to be easier than with a side–by–side. Certainly the view down the barrel is far less cluttered and many people find this an important factor. Again, the design of the gun demands that more wood has to be used in the fore–end, and the stock needs to be deeper to take the deepened action. Couple this with the need to reinforce the sides and frame of the gun's action with extra metal and an altogether heavier gun than a similarly constructed side–by–side is produced. The extra weight has the advantage that it absorbs a greater amount of recoil and this factor was very quickly appreciated by clay pigeon shooters. Single trigger mechanisms, whereby both barrels could be fired by two pulls on the same trigger, were soon incorporated into the design of over–and–under shotguns and this increased its popularity among clay shooters. It was a combination of these factors, however, coupled with the time this design arrived on the general market which made it so popular among the live game shooters of North America.

As stated earlier, the mid 1920's saw the first relatively inexpensive over–and–under shotguns being marketed. By this time the North American arms manufacturers had been producing efficient, automatic loading and repeating shotguns for over two decades and the American shotgunner had certainly developed a liking for the heavier single barrel repeating weapon. A great many of these, in their search for such advantages as an instant choice of chokes or cartridges when hunting, had tried the European style of side–by–side and had found the design difficult to adapt to. The over–and–under provided the ideal solution. Here was a weapon which almost matched the weight of their favourite single barrel repeater, was similarly equipped with one trigger, and had a simple 'one barrel' sighting plane. Nevertheless, the over–and–under had all the advantages of any double barrelled gun in terms of the variety of chokes or loads and it was instantly possible to select.

The general adoption of this gun as a clay pigeon weapon quickly led to a diversification into specialist guns for the different disciplines. Thus over–and–unders for skeet shooting, where targets are broken at close ranges, are usually short barrelled and cylinder or retro–choke bored. A greater than normal drop in the stock which usually has a pistol grip is another feature designed for quick shouldering of the skeet gun, as this is one discipline where the shooter has the gun off the shoulder when the bird is called. On the other hand trap and Olympic trench shooting demanded a very different weapon. The gun is used at rising targets launched away from the shooter so that long range heavily choked barrels are needed. Trap guns are therefore commonly bored full and three–quarters (improved modified) choke. The stock tends to be longer than normal with far less bend, often cut in Monte Carlo style and fitted with a recoil pad. This design of stock is intended to make the weapon shoot higher than the point of aim, a decided advantage when shooting at rising targets. As there is no real need to carry the gun for lengthy periods, trap guns are heavily built, weighing an average of 8 pounds (3.6 kg), and this alone makes this weapon unsuitable for many other shooting situations.

In order to supply the demand for over-and-under guns for game shooting, two styles seem to have evolved. The general purpose field guns, built and bored similarly to the side-by-side field gun, and the true game gun built at a minimum weight with short barrels and open boring. These guns are very often fitted with double triggers, so that in every way except the alignment of barrels, they resemble the more traditional side-by-side game gun. Similarly, magnum wildfowling over-and-under shotguns are also made but these do not seem to be as popular as either the side-by-side or the multi-shot repeaters. One possible explanation for this could be the fact that the extractor and ejector mechanisms of this type of gun, housed on either side of the barrel are exposed every time the gun is opened. In the rigorous and very often muddy conditions associated with coastal wildfowling this can be a decided disadvantage as mud and sand can cause rapid and excessive wear.

It can therefore be seen that double barrel shotguns are available to cover all the different types of shotgun shooting that are encountered in Britain, Europe and North America. A specialist weapon can be obtained for many special shooting situations and the weapon is generally accepted as being versatile enough to be pressed into service in a wider role than could be achieved using a single barrel, single choke gun.

PRODUCING A DOUBLE BARREL GUN

Even though there is a wide variety in the types of double guns available, they are all produced by the same sequence of processes and it is this that I wish to describe next. Basically, there are three main processes involved in the making of a double barrel gun. These, in the sequence in which they are normally carried out, are barrelling, actioning and stocking. To these three can be added a fourth stage, which is called finishing, but this is far less clearly defined than the others.

Barrelling

The quality of any finished shotgun barrel depends to a great extent on three factors. The quality of the steel from which the barrel has been made, the accuracy of the machinery used in the turning and boring of the tubes and the time and care that has been used by the craftsman barreller in boring and polishing the chokes, chambers and the internal bore. In a double barrel gun this is further complicated by the need to align the barrels carefully so that they both shoot to the same point of aim.

Very few manufacturers now take in steel ingots and rough timber at one end of their production line and produce their guns from these basic raw materials. The almost universal present day practice is to purchase rough steel rods from the steel manufacturers. If side-by-side barrels are to be produced, these steel rods also often have a 'lump' at one end which will eventually become the lumps under the barrel which secure the barrel to the action. On rods that are destined to become over-and-under barrels these lumps are usually absent, being brazed on later if they are used at all. On receipt of these rough forgings, the gunmaker's first task is to cut the rod to the required length, after which it can be bored approximately to the required calibre. This is usually a machine process and modern machinery can bore out these tubes to very fine tolerances. The external diameter of the rod is also turned or 'struck' down to the required diameter and the lumps are roughly machined to an approximation of their eventual length and width. The machine operators have to exercise considerable care during the barrel boring process to produce an internal bore that has a uniform diameter and is, above all, straight. It is a general truth, applicable to barrel making as to all other facets of gunmaking, that time spent in careful work is always reflected in the quality of the finished product. Of course this is also reflected in the price, so that it is only the most expensive guns that receive the greatest quota of the craftsman's time and attention.

In most cases the process of boring out the tubes to the required calibre is finished by hand, but the amount of manual work involved depends on either the tolerances of the machine boring or the amount of time the gunmaker is prepared to spend in the more traditional, skilled method of boring by hand. The process of removing the final layer of metal before the true bore diameter is reached is known as 'lapping' and it is at this stage when the chokes and the chambers are also made. Usually, the barrel is made with a maximum amount of choke so that at a later stage it can be regulated to throw more open patterns if required.

By this stage the barrel bears a much closer resemblance to the finished article in that the internal profile is correct and the exterior has been turned down to provide barrels of the correct weight, thickness and strength. These are now polished inside and out and the pairs of barrels are then carefully aligned and brazed together. While considerable attention is given to the alignment among better quality gunmakers, it is at this point that poor or hurried workmanship is first made evident in a gun which throws its two shot loads to different points. Having been brazed together, ribs are then laid between the barrels, and the loop (the device which holds the fore-end in place) is brazed to the underside. The bottom ribs on a side-by-side and the side ribs on an over-and-under have a concave profile but the top rib can show considerable variation in design. The standard side-by-side rib is the concave rib, but guns with sunk ribs, flat file-cut ribs, and even raised ventilated ribs are also made. This last mentioned rib is also the standard sighting rib on the over-and-under, but here again the width of the rib can vary considerably.

Often, when the barrels have reached the stage when they are joined and ribbed, they are subjected to the first or preliminary proof. This means that a charge is fired through them in order to discover any major flaws in the barrel's material or construction. When the test is passed the barrels are ready for joining to the action.

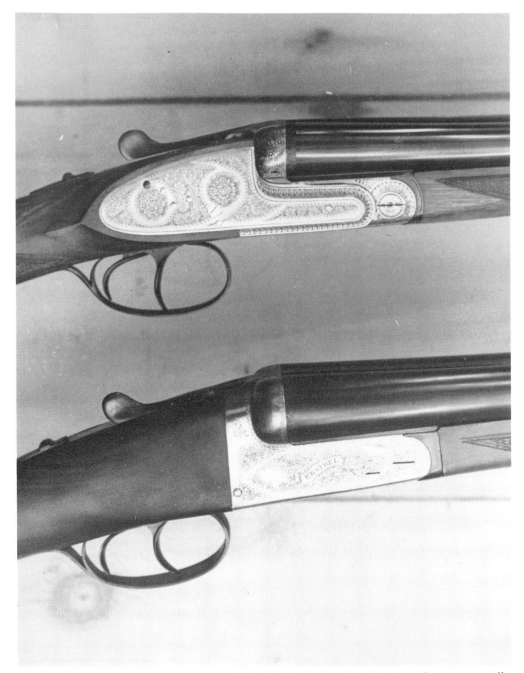

Figure 3.2   Shotgun actions — sidelock (*above*) and boxlock actions are easily
recognised on these European manufactured side-by-side guns

Actioning

The 'action' encompasses the devices for opening and closing the gun, cocking the firing device, firing the gun, and those mechanisms which prevent the gun being inadvertantly fired. In addition to these, guns can be fitted with automatic ejector mechanisms which only throw the fired case clear of the gun. Most guns with double barrels are now made with their opening mechanism operated by a lever on top of the gun — the so called top-lever action. Other double guns are also made with side and under lever actions but these now are restricted to a few small gauge guns, particularly in the .410 calibre. Side-by-side guns are usually designed so that the barrels and action are locked together by means of bolts, which are really metal bars, housed in the action and engaged on slots in the lump to hold the barrels rigidly against the breech face of the action body. Additional strength may be obtained by extending the top rib into a slot in the top of the action and locking it there by a 'cross bolt' or some other device.

We can safely assume, I think, that in the time it has taken for the breech loading gun to evolve to its present state, any weaknesses in the locking of the barrels and action have been eliminated and the guns made today, although their mechanisms show wide variations, are all soundly constructed in this context. The barrels of all double guns are now made to hinge downwards on opening; the only exception I know of, the French Darne 'sliding breech' recently ceased to be produced. If this can be taken as a rather uniquely designed exception, all other double guns can be divided into two categories according to the type of firing mechanism or lock that is used.

The great majority of over-and-under and side-by-side guns are built around the **boxlock** action designed by Anson and Deeley. This action has proved to be simple to build, strong and reliable even under extremes of temperature and humidity, but it does tend to give the gun a rather bulky appearance, hence the term 'boxlock'. In the original design of the lockwork there were only four moving parts. The hammer or tumbler, which also served as the firing pin, the main spring, the cocking lever, and the firing lever or 'sear'. These were housed in the body of the action and this gave the gun a distinct 'cut off' at the join between the action and the stock. All the less expensive guns are made on the boxlock action, as the only other important alternative, the sidelock, is a more complicated mechanism and is, therefore, more expensive to produce.

As its name implies, the locks of the **sidelock** gun are fitted in the side of the action rather than inside the action body. The mechanism is, therefore, more spread out and consequently a slimmer, more graceful weapon is the result. In addition, this design puts a greater area of metal on the surface of the gun, as the lock plates reach as far back as to be in line with the back trigger, so the skilled engraver has much more opportunity to show off his artistic skills. Therefore, all the best guns produced by the most famous English and Continental makers are made to the sidelock pattern. While it is certainly a less robust mechanism than the boxlock it must be remembered that these are purely relative terms and a well made sidelock will easily withstand the most demanding and rigorous conditions without malfunction. If this were not the case no best quality gunmaker would even consider using the design! Unlike the boxlock the locks of the sidelock are more exposed to dirt and dust, so they are often fitted with a small thumb operated screw and are thereby easily removable for cleaning. This is what is meant by the term detachable locks.

Whichever types of locks are used, the basic production methods are the same. The action body and fore-end forgings are received in the rough state and firstly machined to an approximation of the final dimensions. At this stage they are said to be 'roughly machined for actioning' but with the accuracy of modern machinery these forgings can be within a very fine tolerance of the finished product.

Actioning means just what it says: all the working parts are made, put together and fitted into the action so that all the mechanisms operate correctly. It is in this area that there are great differences between the working practice of the 'best' gunmakers and of those producing guns for the lower end of the market. In the workshops of the 'best' London gunmakers, for example, all the working parts of the action are hand made, often by one craftsman and many hours of slow, patient and very skilled work ensure that all parts fit perfectly and operate smoothly. When the action is finally assembled all the working parts are carefully hardened in order to ensure a minimum of wear. From the stage when the forging is machined for actioning, the barrels and action are worked on together to ensure that they are filed and shaped to fit each other perfectly in the finished product. In order to achieve this, one method commonly used is to coat the surfaces that come into contact with one another — the lumps and under bolt, the flats of barrel and action, and the standing breech and the barrel — with soot from a paraffin lamp.

Figure 3.3   Stephen Grant Sidelock 12 bore — a best quality English shotgun
Courtesy: Churchill, Atkin, Grant and Lang Ltd.

When the action and barrels are closed the soot is forced off the 'high spots' and these can then be seen when the working parts are again dismantled. This laborious, but highly skilled, process of 'sooting' and 'filing' continues until all the areas of contact are even.

By this time the tolerances have been reduced to the thickness of one soot grain and it will have taken a considerable time, sometimes a matter of months. Understandably, with such meticulous attention to detail the guns often take up to three years to build and the annual production of a best London gunmaker is consequently a small figure. Holland and Holland, for example, produce about fifty best guns in a year, but their shotguns, like those from Purdey or Boss are generally considered to be the finest in the world and are often taken as the weapons by which others are judged. At the other end of the scale there are many large arms manufacturers in Europe which specialise in producing double barrel shotguns. Firms such as AyA and Laurona in Spain and Bernadelli in Italy have, over the past twenty or so years, built up a very good reputation for producing low priced but very soundly built and reliable shotguns. In these firms' factories, many of the traditional and time consuming tasks have been streamlined by the use of modern and high precision machinery. The fine tolerances that these machines can work to cuts down on the time required for hand finishing any component and production is therefore much faster. These, it must be remembered, are large organisations which produce large numbers of weapons each year. AyA, for instance, employs more skilled craftsmen than the whole of the English gun trade and its annual output of shotguns may run into six figures.

This mass production can only stem from extensive use of machines to carry out as many of the gunmaking tasks as possible. Most parts of an action are stamped out of sheet metal and are only finished by hand. Machines that can polish over fifty lock plates in a total time of fifteen minutes demonstrate the extent of mechanisation, so that the craftsman assembling the action may only need to spend a short time putting it together and checking the operation of the components. With so many craftsmen available, however, the top models of the manufacturer's range, sidelock ejector guns built only to special order, reflect the same skills and care that the English gunmakers exercise in producing their best guns. Many manufacturers in Italy and Spain have, therefore, built up respectable reputations for the reliability of their cheap models, and craftsmanship embodied in their best guns.

When the action and barrels have been fitted together to the satisfaction of the gunmaker, the whole assembly is usually submitted for proof in order to test its ability to stand up to above normal pressures. This proof test thereby leaves a good safety margin for the shotgun's owner when the weapon is loaded with the cartridges for which it was designed. After the proof test and subsequent inspection are complete, the proof marks are stamped on the barrel flats and the action, and the whole assembly is ready for stocking.

Stocking

First the rough shape of the stock is cut from a solid block of wood, in most cases this is walnut but sometimes other varieties of hardwood are used. For the best guns the stock blanks are selected for their grain markings, it is only natural that the better guns are allocated the well figured and closer grained timber for their stocks. When the block has been roughly cut to the shape of the stock and a matching fore-end block has been similarly shaped, the action end is carefully curved and inletted to accept the action body and lockwork. The boxlock action is a relatively straightforward mechanism to fit onto a stock, and an accurate wood to metal fit is quite easily obtainable. This close fitting is important in that, as well as having a neat and pleasing appearance, the continuous wood to metal contact evenly distributes the recoil force when the gun is fired. A poorly fitting action can often set up abnormally high stresses in the stock and cause it to fracture or warp.

Fitting a sidelock action is a far more delicate and precise exercise. Sufficient wood must be cut away to enable the locks to operate freely, but removal of two much wood tends to weaken the stock at this point. There is a far greater amount of metal to wood contact, so that achieving a good fit is correspondingly more difficult. Traditionally, the side-by-side shotgun action, whether boxlock or sidelock, is secured to the stock by means of screws from the top and bottom strap of the action, but many manufacturers now employ the method that is widely used in over-and-under guns of reinforcing this with a stock bolt which runs through the stock and threads into the rear of the action body.

When the action has been properly fitted, the stock is shaped first by cutting, then filing and finally sanding, to the desired style and dimensions. Having done this, the complete gun is assembled and the stock is hollowed and weighted in order to produce a better balanced weapon.

Finishing

By now the shotgun can be assembled and fired, but work on it is not yet complete. At this stage the gun is referred to as being 'in the white' and is ready for finishing. The barrels are blacked and polished, a sighting bead is fitted to the rib and the operation of the extractors is eased. The stock and fore-end are chequered, either by machine or by hand, and the wood is stained and protected in a variety of ways. Many of the less expensive guns are marketed with polyurethane varnished stocks and fore-ends but a semi-matt oil finish is more widely used and traditional. When the gun is in the white it receives the attention of the gunmaker's engraver, and this is the first opportunity during the process of building the gun for a certain amount of artistic flair to be used. Many guns never receive the attention of an engraver, however, as there are three main ways in which a gun's action can be decorated.

The simplest form of engraving is performed by a stamping machine, which actually stamps a pattern on the appropriate part of the action. Many of the cheapest guns are embellished in this way and some of the decorations that are produced are simple but quite elegant and certainly add to the appearance of the gun. Obviously it is easier to stamp a pattern onto a flat surface, so that actions decorated in this way often have curved surfaces left here.

More complicated in certain respects is a process known as chemical etching. A corrosive compound is applied to the action in such a way as to eat into the metal's surface in a strictly controlled pattern. When this process is completed a variety of 'pictures' stand out as relief against the areas where the metal has been removed and this again can produce pleasing and quite elegant decoration on a gun's action.

Finally, hand engraving is the type of decoration which is considered to be better than either of the others in terms of the quality and appearance of the finished article. Hand engraving shows a considerable variation in style; at the simplest end of the scale is the type known as 'border engraving' and at the other end is the ornate gold and pearl inlay. Obviously as one travels up the price scale, so the type of engraving becomes an increasingly skilled and artistic operation. The best quality guns of any manufacturer usually have delicately and tastefully engraved actions which, while adding nothing to the gun's shooting qualities, certainly increases the aesthetic beauty of the weapon. Most manufacturers of good quality guns offer a 'custom engraving' service whereby the customer can specify the type of decoration he requires. Game scenes are popular, as is, for those who can afford it, gold inlay. It is probably true to say that a well engraved best gun is not only a smoothly operating efficient weapon, but it is also a work of art.

After all the decorative work is done the action is finished, either by polishing to brightness or colour hardened to give a beautiful mottled appearance. The gun is now finally assembled and test fired to regulate the pattern. The amount of time

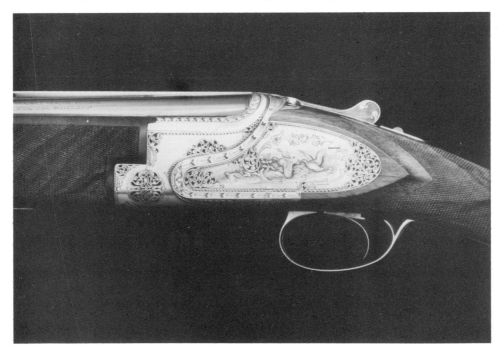

Figure 3.4   Skilled and artistic engraving seen on dummy side plates of Browning F1 grade over-and-under
Courtesy: Browning (UK) Ltd.

spent on this again varies between makers and depends on the quality of the guns produced. A low priced gun is usually test fired only to ascertain that the patterns conform to the choke borings, but best guns are taken much further than this. Patterns are checked for density, evenness of dispersion and consistency of performance and many hours may still be spent regulating the chokes. The final phase is the pre-delivery check to ensure that the gun is operating correctly. The gun is then ready for the customer.

MANUFACTURERS

Britain

It is probably true to say that there are now no inexpensive double barrel shotguns produced in Britain. More than any other gunmaking nation the gunmakers of London, Birmingham and other provincial towns have refused to give up many of the traditional gunmaking skills which elsewhere have been superseded by machinery. Consequently there are no firms in Britain that can match some of the European and American manufacturers in terms of total output, and the largely handbuilt British shotgun caters for a rather exclusive market. Britain's largest shotgun producing firm, W. C. Scott of Birmingham, also market a less expensive range of English guns in their boxlock ejectors. Even so, the price of this gun puts it in the medium price bracket where it competes successfully with many fine quality sidelock guns from Mediterranean Europe.

The shooting fraternity, as has been demonstrated many times in the shotgun's history, tends to let old ideas die very slowly and the appeal of owning an 'English Gun', stemming from the time when these were indisputably the finest available, is still very strong. The British gunmakers' reluctance to abandon traditional hand skills does still mean that their guns live up to the reputation of the past so, while they have lost the lower end of the market to the less expensive continental gunmakers, they are happy to supply the upper end of the market with exclusive custom built weapons. Very few British shotguns can be bought 'off the shelf', the majority being made to order. Therefore, the gun can be made to fit the individual purchaser in its stock length, cast, bend, and design. Engraving and barrel boring can be carried out to personal taste and the gun regulated to shoot a particular load with maximum efficiency.

As a step up from the boxlock-only makers, such as W.C. Scott, we come to those that offer a range of both boxlock and sidelock. Such firms as William Powell, and Westley Richards in Birmingham, Lindseys in Leeds and Cogswell & Harrison in London make guns which vary from medium priced boxlocks to 'best' sidelocks. At the top of the scale, of course, are the firms that really specialise in best guns, such as Boss, Holland & Holland, and Purdey. Throughout this range the gunmakers are aware that the intense competition from Europe demands that their guns never lose the quality upon which their reputations are based. It is safe to say, therefore, that any English made double shotgun has quality built in.

The great majority of British guns are made as side-by-sides, but some gunmakers, Boss and Purdey in particular, also make over-and-under guns to

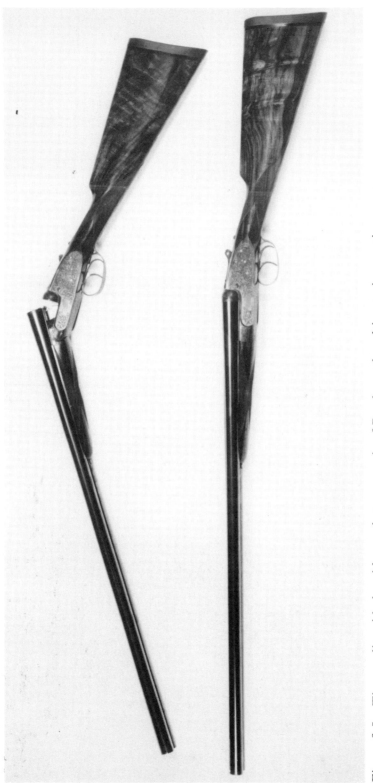

Figure 3.5   The quality side by side market — a pair of Purdeys, the ultimate in sporting guns

Courtesy: J. Purdey and Sons

special order. These weapons are regarded by many people to be the ultimate in clay pigeon guns, just as their side-by-sides are looked upon as the ultimate game guns.

Europe

In terms of the size of the individual gunmaking firms, and the quality of guns that they produce, Europe shows a much greater degree of contrast. There, the gunmaking industry can be divided into four main categories by defining the variety, quality and scale of output. There are, as has already been mentioned, a number of large companies which produce the complete range of weapons from the least expensive non-ejector boxlock to custom built sidelocks. AyA, Laurona and Ugartachea, all based in Spain, are good examples of the first category.

There are also other large scale producers of shotguns who direct their products more towards the middle and upper markets. Often, these companies, in addition to producing double guns, also produce a variety of repeating weapons. Fabrique Nationale of Belgium concentrate their production on a wide range of over-and-under sold under the Browning name, although they are justifiably famous for their repeating guns. The same can be said of Beretta, and Luigi Franchi, both Italian companies, who although they do produce side-by-sides, concentrate production on over-and-unders and repeaters. Other gunmakers to fall into this category include Verney-Carron in France and Merkel and Sauer in Germany, who produce a wide range of double guns of both types.

Figure 3.6   Modern double gun — large quantities of side by side, semi-hammerless .410 shotguns like this are still produced in Belgium and Spain

Then there are the small scale, highly skilled gunmakers, who resemble the English maker in many respects. These produce guns to individual design, and their quality, which stems from long traditions in making high class weapons, ranks as equal to their English counterparts. Meticulously made and exquisitely engraved guns by such makers as Famars, Fabbri, and Zanotti have won world acclaim, and the artistic skill that goes into the engraving cannot be bettered anywhere in the world.

The final category of European gunmaker is composed of the firms, large or small, which concentrate on the production of inexpensive weapons. In no way should these be decried merely on the grounds of their low price. Weapons from Zalaba, Jabali and Gorosabel, for example, have earned a good reputation for their hard wearing and reliable qualities. Modern machinerey and the large labour force in Spain and Italy serve to keep the production costs as low as possible and this is reflected in the price of the guns that are made. Generally speaking the best guns produced by the European makers compare very favourably with their English counterparts, and the cheapest guns they make serve to provide reliable and hard wearing weapons for a much wider section of the shooting public.

North America

At the present time most double barrel shotguns used in North America are imported either from Europe, Japan, or increasingly, Brazil. The great majority of American shotgun production concentrates on the classic 'American Gun', the Auto-loading and repeating guns, but a small number of the larger manufacturers do produce a range of double guns. Of these the over–and–under makes up the vast bulk of the output, and the American built side–by–side is a rare weapon indeed!

The outstanding difference between the European and American arms manufacturers lies in the fact that most European guns are made for export, whereas most American guns are made for the home market. The popularity of the over–and–under as a game gun in America I have already explained and this is reflected in the fact that this type of gun is the only double barrel shotgun produced by such well established makers as Weatherby and Remington. Winchester, Savage, and Browning in addition produce a wide range of over–and–under guns, and it is these last three organisations which also make a limited range of side-by-side shotguns.

Considering the American shotgunner's liking for a heavier gun, a single sighting line and a wider grip for the leading hand, it is only natural that a distinctly American style of side-by-side should evolve. These side-by-sides, therefore, look very different to the typical English lightweight sporting gun, in that they have full pistol grip stocks, single trigger mechanisms, large 'beaver tail' fore-ends and a raised ventilated rib. A European gunmaker exporting his products to both Britain and North America will, therefore, probably build two completely different styles of weapon from the same barrel and action forgings. Each would be designed to suit the preferences of their market destination; this highlights the futility of the often published arguments as to which style of gun is the better to use. Every individual shooter will eventually find the combination of cartridge and style of gun that will best suit him or her, and the choice of these is a very personal factor.

One fact, however, cannot really be argued against. The double barrel shotgun, in all its diverse forms and variations, is the most commonly used smooth bore weapon throughout the world.

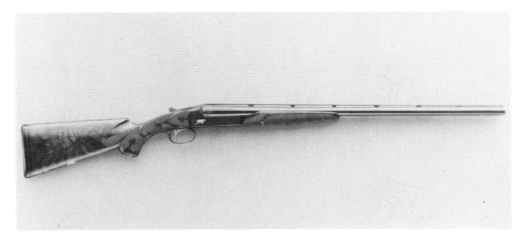

Figure 3.7   American style double-Winchester Model 21, typical of American side by sides with its raised, ventilated rib, pistol grip stock and beavertail fore-end
Courtesy: Winchester-Western

4
Repeating and Automatic-Loading Shotguns

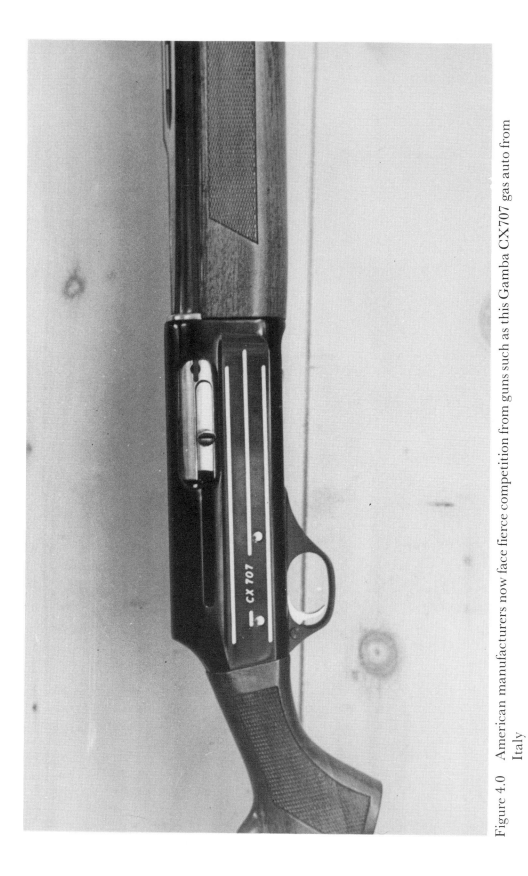

Figure 4.0   American manufacturers now face fierce competition from guns such as this Gamba CX707 gas auto from Italy

Repeating and Automatic-Loading Shotguns

While the double-barrel shotgun is very much a European weapon with an ancestry that reaches back to the early 19th century, the single barrel multi-shot shotgun is definitely a style of weapon born and nurtured in North America around the beginning of this century. Even before that time attempts were made, in Britain and Europe as well as America, to increase the fire power of the shotgun. Prior to the appearance of the first successful auto-loading and pump action shotguns, Charles Lancaster, an English gunmaker had designed and built four-barrelled shotguns, Samuel Colt had produced a revolver action single barrel shotgun, and even a belt-fed repeating percussion shotgun, firing a belt of fourteen charges had been produced.

All these early attempts failed. The multi-barrelled and belt-fed guns were too heavy and cumbersome, the revolving chambered gun suffered from gas leakage between the chamber and barrel, and, at that time, the firms that did produce these prototype repeaters did not really have the engineering skill to overcome the problems. By around 1910, however, due largely to the genius of people like John M. Browning, the first really successful multi-shot single barrel weapons were in production by such makers as Remington, Winchester, Marlin, Savage and Stevens in North America and Fabrique National in Belgium.

Today there are three main types of repeating multi shot weapons. The 'automatic', or more correctly **automatic-loading** shotguns, and **pump**, or slide action, gun I have already described briefly; the third category consists of the **bolt action repeating gun**.

MANUFACTURERS

Although the great bulk of weapons in all three categories are produced by the famous North American firms such as Winchester, Remington, Ithaca, Savage-Stevens Marlin, a number of other gun producing countries in Europe and Asia now make a variety of these shotguns which compete for the predominantly American market. Among the European gunmakers, Manufrance and Fabrique Nationale in France and Belgium, Beretta, Franchi and Breda in Italy and a

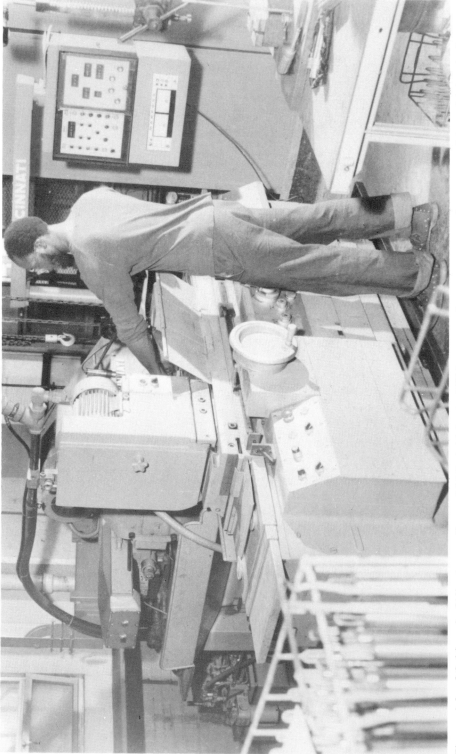

Figure 4.1 Making the Winchester Super X Model 1 in the USA — a workman operates the new machine which grinds the outside diameter of the barrel extension of the shotgun

Courtesy: Winchester–Western

Figure 4.2   Automatic shotgun reproduction — special numerically controlled machine which cuts the checkering on both stock and forearm of Winchester Super X Model 1 shotgun

Courtesy: Winchester–Western

number of smaller firms, produce a variety of autos, pumps and bolt action repeaters which, alongside Japanese guns from S.K.B. and K.F.C., are taking an increasingly significant share of the American gun market.

Despite all the technological advances which have affected the way in which these guns are manufactured, the original concept which caused these weapons to evolve has not really been lost. Even though manufacturers now show considerable variations in the design of their guns, they are still basically simple weapons which have a far greater number of machine-hours than man-hours in their construction. They are the product of a capital-intensive rather than a labour-intensive industry. Many still conform to the original demands made of this type of shotgun, in that they are easy to field-strip without tools, making them easy to maintain and clean, and the reliability can be judged by the fact that the basic designs laid down in the early 1900's have not needed to be changed since.

THE BOLT ACTION

Of the three basic types, the bolt action repeater is perhaps the simplest and certainly the cheapest to manufacture. This type of gun had been produced since the early years of this century, but the earliest examples of European origin generally gave the marque a bad name. Before the Second World War, however, Savage and Stevens were producing cheap but well made bolt action shotguns, though nowadays guns by these makers compete with those by Mossberg, Marlin and a small number of European makers who produce similar weapons.

Bolt action repeating shotguns are made in a variety of gauges and configurations, though they all tend to be three shot clip-fed weapons. There are one or two exceptions to this as some models produced by Harrington and Richardson, J.C. Higgins, and Stevens have been six shot tubular magazine fed, the magazine being placed under the barrel. These, however, have confined their production to the .410 gauge, as a 12 bore of similar tube-fed bolt action design would not compete favourably with other designs with similar fire power.

Perhaps because of their cheapness, lack of elegance (compared to other shotgun designs) and simplicity, the bolt action repeater has come under a great deal of criticism from a number of authorities; yet it is their simplicity that is their greatest advantage. Any bolt action weapon, be it shotgun or rifle, has comparatively few moving parts, so that malfunctions and mechanical breakdowns are very rare occurrences. They are an excellent means, therefore, by which a shooter can obtain a very reliable weapon for a low cost. It has to be admitted that the rate of fire is slower than either of the other multi shot weapons or a double gun, but there are a great many shooting situations when this is not really an important factor. Even so, a bolt action shotgun user can, with practice, achieve a rapid loading system. I have a farmer friend who can regularly take two birds out of a covey of driven partridge when using his son's .410 bolt action repeater. Despite the shortcomings, real or imagined, that people believe a gun of this design to have, I think they are ideal weapons for informal shooting, such as pest destruction. Their versatility can be increased by the addition of some sort of variable choke device, which will be described later in this chapter, and they can then become good general purpose guns. One manufacturer has even developed three highly specialised bolt action guns for particular types of shooting. Marlin now market two specialist, three shot bolt action wildfowling weapons as the 12 gauge 'Goose Gun' and the 10 gauge 'Super Goose'. These heavy weapons, fitted with the extra long and heavily choked barrels needed for flighting or 'pass' shooting, have become established as reliable, hard hitting, and inexpensive weapons and are, understandably, popular.

Their other specialist bolt action is built to the same basic design in 12 gauge, but sports a 20 inch (50 cm) improved cylinder barrel with rifle type sights, and the action is even drilled and tapped for 'scope mounting'. This they call their 'slug gun' and is the specialist weapon for the close cover and woodland deer hunter in North America, or the wild boar hunter in Europe.

THE PUMP ACTION

The first really successful pump or slide action shotgun appeared in 1893 and was manufactured by Winchester. This was followed in 1897 with probably the most popular pump action of all time, the Winchester 97. Both these guns were designed by John M. Browning, a man who was to distinguish himself even further a few years later. The general operating principle of his pump action designs have remained unchanged to the guns produced today. The gun is loaded by a back and

Figure 4.3   The Marlin 10-bore — a 3 shot bolt action repeater
Courtesy: Marlin Co.

forward movement of the bolt, which lifts a cartridge from the tubular magazine beneath the barrel and guides it into the chamber. This movement is accomplished by means of a sliding fore-end or fore-arm. As it moves to the rear the bolt lock is disengaged and the fired cartridge is extracted from the chamber and ejected. When the fore-end reaches the rearward end of its travel the bolt is wide open and a cartridge is lifted from the magazine. At this point the gun is also cocked ready to fire the next round which is fed into the chamber by the forward movement of the bolt, brought about by the forward movement of the fore-end. At the end of its forward travel the bolt is locked into position so that it cannot accidentally open as the gun is fired and this lock is only released by recoil, or by the release of the trigger after it has been pulled to fire the gun.

The early Winchester was built with an external hammer, but by 1912 Winchester were producing their hammerless Model 12. By that time also, other American manufacturers including Marlin, Stevens, Remington, and Savage were also producing pump action shotguns of similar design. Nowadays the pump action gun usually has a capacity for five shots at one loading, that is, one cartridge in the chamber and four in the magazine, although some makers can supply an extension magazine to increase capacity to seven shots. All makers of these weapons also supply magazine plugs which restrict capacity to three shots in order to comply with hunting regulations in many parts of the world. With one or two exceptions pump guns eject the cartridge either to the left or the right of the action, but both Remington and Ithaca have produced bottom ejecting shotguns; the Ithaca model 37 being particularly successful. Each manufacturer, at present, makes and

Figure 4.4   Glenfield 778, a typical pump action shotgun

markets a wide variety of pump action shotguns, and guns of this type can be obtained in every gauge from .410 to 12 and in every grade from plain to luxury. Since the birth of this weapon many makers have made great efforts to produce a more graceful gun, and nowadays guns like the Weatherby Patrician and Winchester 1200 have clean and elegant lines which belie their strength and ruggedness.

In all but the most demanding circumstances these weapons can reload and fire as quickly as any autoloading shotgun, and some users claim that they are more effective, because the act of pushing forward the slide during reloading helps to stabilise the aim after a shot has been taken. In North America the guns are a popular choice for all forms of shooting, from upland quail to coastal wildfowling, and the variety of gauges and models available from the great manufacturers of these guns reflect this wide range of shooting sports. Although few countries outside the U.S.A. have produced shotguns to the pump action design, France stands out in that it manufactures the 'Rapid' shotgun which sells well in Europe. It appears that no large scale European manufacturer has attempted to break into the American market in pump guns, but when one considers the high quality of the American products, it is perhaps not really surprising. More than either the bolt action or auto-loading shotgun, the pump action is a shotgun style in which American arms manufacturers dominate the world.

THE SELF-LOADER OR 'AUTOMATIC'

Compared to either of the two repeaters already described, the self loading shotgun has undergone a much greater degree of evolution from its prototype. In 1905 the first successful automatic loading shotgun, the gun that was to make its designer John M. Browning a household name, was manufactured in Europe by Fabrique Nationale of Belgium and by Remington in North America. The mechanism, which has come to be called the long recoil system, operated on the principle that the energy of the recoil could provide the power to reload and recock the weapon in one simple, if violent, movement. On firing the gun, the barrel and breech block recoil about 3 inches (7.6 cm). At the end of the recoil stroke the barrel and breech disengage, the barrel begins its forward travel and the empty cartridge is thereby extracted. When the barrel reaches its forward-most position a fresh cartridge is fed upwards from the tube magazine below and takes the place of the empty case which is ejected. The breech block then travels forward on its return spring and the firing mechanism is cocked before the breech again locks itself into the barrel with a new round in the chamber ready for firing; the whole process taking about one-tenth of a second. For the first time it was possible to fire five rounds of a shotgun as fast as the trigger could be pulled, though, of course, there were few circumstances when this was ever necessary. Browning protected his patents so well that it was only in 1911 that Winchester could produce its first autoloading shotgun. From that date to the early 1950's practically every self loader was modelled on Browning's original and these copies were not, like the pump action guns, confined to the American firms. As well as F.N. in Belgium,

Breda of Italy produced a restyled automatic which gained rapidly in popularity.

In 1954 Winchester produced the first weapon to depart from Browning's long recoil action in which the barrel is fixed and the energy required for the reloading sequence was obtained from a short rearward movement, about $\frac{1}{10}$ inch (0.25 cm), of a 'floating chamber'. This short movement, through a rather complex system of weights and buffers, was enough to send the breech block far enough back to eject the empty case and feed a new one into the chamber from below. Because there was less movement in the heavy components of the gun during reloading the new design did not suffer the inertia problems encountered in the long recoil gun and it was an immediate success.

GAS OPERATED AUTOMATIC

Just one year later, J.C. Higgins produced the model 60 shotgun on yet another type of mechanism. Taking the idea behind the English Bren light machine gun and the American Garand Rifle, this firm produced the first gas operated auto–loading shotgun. In this mechanism a small portion of the rapidly expanding gases which are produced by a cartridge being fired is tapped off through a small hole, or exhaust port, in the barrel wall. This gas enters an expansion chamber and drives a piston which, after a specified time delay, in turn operates the breech block. This delay allows the shot charges to be well clear of the gun with a consequent safe residual gas pressure in the barrel before the breech is unlocked.

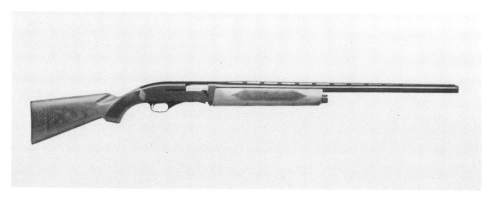

Figure 4.5   Winchester Model 1400 — typical of the American style of gas auto
Courtesy: Winchester-Western

This system had considerable advantages over the recoil operated systems, the main one being that recoil was virtually eliminated and there was a distinct absence of the long recoil's shuffle movement when the gun was fired.

In 1956 Remington following Higgins' example and marketed their first departure from recoil autos as their gas operated 58. The one disadvantage of this type of weapon is that different cartridges can produce different gas pressures and thus the operation of the mechanism can be affected. In order to compensate for this, the Remington 'Sportsman 58' had a gas pressure adjuster placed on the top of the magazine tube cap which could be set for light or heavy load shells; subsequent models have been developed with automatic adjusters, so that nowadays a mixture of heavy and light cartridges may be fired at one loading.

In the development of the gas auto, American arms manufacturers have led the way, with perhaps the best seller of all guns of this type being the Remington Model 1100. At the present time practically all the autoloading shotguns produced in America are gas operated, while a large proportion of those produced in Europe and, increasingly Japan are recoil operated. There is however, a change coming about as F.N. now produce their gas model 2000 alongside their traditional square backed recoil auto, and Manufrance is now concentrating its output on a 4 shot gas auto. Perhaps the most important European country for auto production is Italy, with its output from the Breda, Benelli, and Franchi organisations. Again, much of their output is still recoil operated, but Franchi in particular is producing high quality weapons of both recoil and gas operation, employing probably the most modern machinery techniques in the world. It is this company which has for

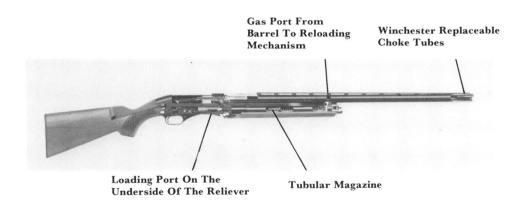

Figure 4.6   Cut away of Winchester Model 1400

example, pioneered the use of swage chokes in their guns. In the light of modern trends it seems reasonable to assume that the gas powered auto is the weapon of the future and it will eventually supersede the recoil models.

If I can, for convenience, group the contemporary pump action and auto loading shotguns together, the group so formed gains most of its popular support in North America, where it has evolved a great number of styles to suit the shooting conditions on that continent. These guns are manufactured in all gauges from .410 to 12 bore and there is even a gas operated 10 bore on the market. The style of gun generally accepted by American upland shooters has a short barrel of between 26 to 28 inches (66–71 cm) and is bored improved cylinder or modified choke. It is therefore ideal for quick pointing close shooting situations such as quail shooting.

The specialist **wildfowl guns** are the opposite. They are more heavily built to absorb magnum recoil, have tightly choked barrels of 30 or more inches (76 cm) in length to make them 'swinging' rather than 'pointing' guns. As just mentioned, Ithaca produce the ultimate in heavy wildfowling weaponry in their 'Mag 10' gas operated 10 gauge shotgun. In a way such a weapon makes a mockery of the Federal restrictions on the bore of a gun, as it has considerably more fire–power than the traditional English 'fowling' piece, the double 8 bore. It is rightly described as the ideal contemporary gun for long range goose shooting.

The various **clay pigeon shooting** disciplines have also caused the evolution of specialist guns. For trap shooting the weapon bears a superficial resemblance to the duck gun having a long and well choked barrel, but unlike the duck gun it also features a high monte-carlo style stock in order to compensate for the rising targets. Skeet guns are short barrelled and open bored, much as the upland guns are, and indeed, their roles are interchangeable. The fact that the automatics in all their configurations produce less noticeable recoil than fixed breech guns has given auto. users a distinct advantage in the field of large clay pigeon competitions and a significant number of autos, and gas autos in particular, are produced for competition purposes.

One of the main advantages of the automatic and pump action gun over conventional doubles is that the barrels are readily, and relatively cheaply, interchangeable. Therefore the user of one of these guns can have a specialist duck gun, deer gun, and skeet gun merely by owning the action stock and fore-end together with a number of barrels. One of the disadvantages claimed by the opponents of this system is that the different barrel lengths alter the balance of the gun, but this can now be answered by the use of only one barrel fitted with a system of choke adjustment.

VARIABLE CHOKE DEVICES

In order to increase the versatility of what is, after all, a single barrel gun by varying the degree of choke in the barrel, three main types of variable choke system have evolved. Firstly there is the fixed attachment on the gun's muzzle, which alters the degree of shot spread by a collet device in which the degree of constriction of the leaves can be varied. One of the earliest and still highly popular examples of this type of device is the Poly-choke. At the muzzle, the choke device is fitted with a ring which is rotated to the desired choke setting for the type of shooting that is expected. With such a device the shooter gains far greater versatility from a single barrel gun, but pattern quality often suffers to some extent. It stands to reason that a variable construction device cannot possibly produce the same consistency of pattern as a carefully bored and regulated choke cone, but nevertheless the performance is satisfactory for most shooting situations and the added versatility far outweighs this disadvantage.

There are also devices which are designed to close down the choking for a second shot, thus automatically varying the choke between the first and the second barrel much in the same way as a conventional double gun. The Choke-matic and the Poly-matic work in this way, firing the first shot at say, half choke then closing down to full choke for the next. Though not as popular as the straightforward Poly-choke, these are certainly ingenious designs which try to produce 'double barrel' performance through one barrel. The Cutts Compensator system is one of the oldest types available. In this design a recoil reducing compensator tube is fixed into the muzzle and further tubes are screwed into this. Manufactured by Lyman, there are six fixed choke tubes and a collet type adjustable tube.

The advantage of the fixed choke tubes is that they can be machined to produce consistent patterns to a standard not possible with an adjustable collet, but the disadvantage is that changing choke tubes is very much more time consuming. In all, there is very little to choose between them, both types provide a great deal of versatility and throw patterns that are generally acceptable, so the choice of which type to fit to a single barrel gun falls very much to personal preference. One criticism, however, is worth noting. The addition of a few ounces, in the form of these devices, to the front of the gun does nothing to help the overall balance of the weapon, and with this in mind some choke manufacturers are understandably reluctant to fit their devices to long barrelled guns. Even with the use of modern light-weight alloys this problem still exists and it is this that has led to the development of the 'in-barrel choke tube'.

This recent development has been taken up by many arms manufacturers as standard equipment on their single barrel repeating shotguns. Winchester, for example, market their 1500 XTR auto and 1300 XTR pump shotguns with their Winchoke tubes. These screw into, rather than onto the muzzle and therefore add no more weight to the front of the gun than any conventional factor choked barrel. Like the Lyman choke tubes, the Winchokes can be carefully regulated to throw very consistent patterns, and when fitted are invisible, apart from a narrow knurled band around the gun's muzzle.

The one remaining disadvantage of choke tubes is that changing them is slow, but nevertheless all the variable choke devices described above allow any single barrel gun to be adapted for a wide variety of shooting situations. This, I believe, far outweighs any of their disadvantages.

CUSTOM GUNS

As well as being produced in a wide variety of gauge and choke combinations, the pump action and autoloading manufacturers also produce a number of 'grades'. This refers to the amount of decoration on the weapon and has no bearing on how the weapon handles and shoots. The cheapest factory produced grade is known as the standard, and deluxe grades are named in a variety of ways from that point. Thus, one manufacturer may use the terms custom grade, pigeon grade, Grand American, in a different order to another. Customising a standard weapon at the factory may involve using a specially selected stock, engraving of varying intricacy and artistry, and even inlaying of precious metals, in order to fulfil the requirements of a particular sportsman. Though this also occurs with double guns, it is the large expanse of 'bare metal' on the receiver sides of a pump or automatic shotgun that really gives a skilled engraver a great deal of scope. Many of the best engraved guns are really works of art, as well as being functional weapons. In addition to the various grades supplied by the manufacturers, North America is the centre of the private customising industry which provides individual clients with a customising service for their weapons. Nothing like it exists anywhere else in the world: perhaps it is only natural of a gun industry which, as stated earlier, is geared to the machine made product. In a country where the reliable mass produced weapon is the norm, a great many hunters like to 'personalise' their guns. Given the right amount of time, and of course the appropriate fee, a standard grade shotgun can be turned into a thing of true artistic beauty. Some of the specimens I have seen have defied description in the sheer artistry and skill the engraver has demonstrated. Though some of these customising firms are quite large, here the name Pachmayr of Los Angeles springs to mind, the vast majority are small one or two man businesses and the work they do is exactly tailored to each client. Masterpieces produced by such people a John Rahner, Don Glaser and Max Bruehl will last as long as the great British and European engravers and they command equal respect for their talents.

The repeating shotgun, in all its many forms, is seen to be very definitely a North American weapon. Of course nowadays the shotguns of this type produced in Europe and Asia are providing the American gun producers with some serious competition on their home ground and, for the sake of progress, this can only be a good thing. In Europe the repeater is gaining in popularity, and even in Britain, that stronghold of the side-by-side double, the single barrel multi-shot weapon has gained a foothold.

Designed to be reliable, robust and cheap, the multi-shot shotgun, be it auto-loading, pump, or bolt action, has achieved its aim and is very much an established sporting weapon. For this, the North American arms manufacturers, and the genius of John M. Browning, must take most of the credit.

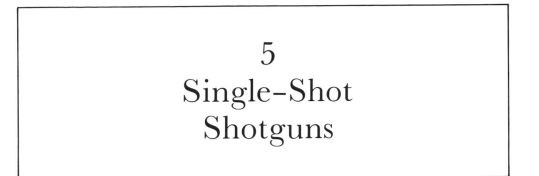

5
Single–Shot
Shotguns

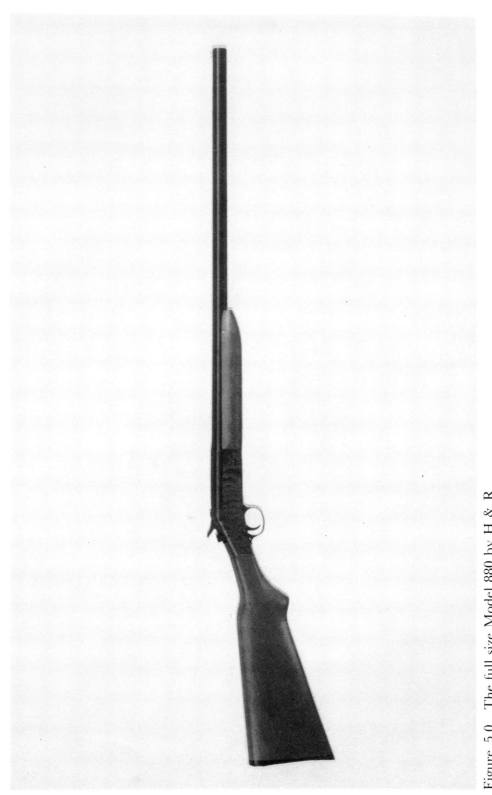

Figure 5.0   The full size Model 880 by H & R

Courtesy: Harrington and Richardson

Single-Shot Shotguns

In the first chapter I gave a chronological account of how we have arrived at the present day designs of shotgun. In the subsequent chapters I have perhaps worked the opposite way, in that I have described the most intricate shotgun first, now finishing up by describing the simplest form at present being manufactured. I have done so because the double-barrel gun, a style of weapon that requires the greatest amount of hand finishing, is the most universally popular type, the machine-made and, therefore, less complicated repeaters and automatics have less of a following and the simple single-shot weapon is certainly the least popular of all shotgun types.

Although the shotgun users of Europe, and particularly of Britain, appear to have a certain prejudice against repeating and automatic guns, there is a far greater prejudice among shotgun users against the single shot weapon. These simple weapons are often relegated very much to the 'second best' category by a great many shooters, who really ought to know better. The idea that a single-shot gun can only be considered as a beginner's weapon seems to stem from the old fallacy that greater accuracy is developed in the learner because he only has one shot at any particular target. The truth is that the newcomer to the sport is far more likely to need a second chance to kill a bird wounded by the first shot. I know my own bags would sometimes be considerably lighter if I did not have the second chance, and a great many more birds would escape to die a slow and painful death. Viewed in this light the single-shot weapon should be the arm of the 'dead shot', rather than of the beginner who is likely to wound more birds than he kills.

DECLINE OF THE SINGLE SHOT

Historically, the original sporting gun was capable of only one shot, and when the first double guns appeared they met with considerable resistance from the shooting public before they were finally accepted. The single-barrelled design continued to be made in all calibres, but especially in the larger wildfowling guns or 'fowling pieces' which continued to be used throughout the last century. The additional weight of a double gun in one of the large bores, made what was already a heavy weapon even more difficult to handle. As the large bores declined, and the European and American gun industries developed more efficient multi-shot weapons of all types, the single-shot weapon fell into disuse as a sporting gun.

It was really from this time onwards that the single-shot weapon was considered as the 'poor man's choice' or the learner's gun as, despite all the advances made in the more popular and fashionable shotgun styles, there were still large quantities of inexpensive single-shot guns being made for the lower end of the market. This type of gun contrasted quite markedly with some of the single guns that had been made previously. In the last years of the 19th century some of the single shotguns produced were built to the 'best' quality, intended probably for the lady shot or the son of a sporting gentleman. By the 1930's the single barrel gun was being made to a minimum quality and price and it therefore reached a far wider section of the sporting public in Britain, Europe and North America. These guns, though made as cheaply as possible, nevertheless were strong, reliable and sufficiently durable to provide the pot hunter with years of satisfactory service. Many of these weapons are still with us today, which is, in itself, a testimony of their qualities.

USES OF THE SINGLE-SHOT

The use to which single-shot weapons are put can be broken down into three categories. The role of 'learner's gun' has already been mentioned, and for this the weapon is usually built in one of the smaller gauges. This, of course assists in keeping the gun light enough to be easily handled by a small child, and a recoil pad is often fitted in order to cushion the shock of the standard loads being fired through what is, after all, a very light weapon. With such a gun the young enthusiast can learn all the skills required of him (or her) as a shotgun user in adult life: stance, gun mounting, accuracy, and above all safety can all be learned by a child using one of these simple and robust shotguns.

Many single-shot guns are produced to the same simple design but in 12 bore size. These are usually intended for use by either the adult new to the sport of shotgun shooting, or by a sportsman who shoots so infrequently that the expense of a more costly repeater or double is not justified. This is the weapon of the so-called casual shooter, who takes the odd day off to have the occasional shot at whatever quarry species he is likely to find in his area. The major advantages of these guns, as with the previous categories, are that they are inexpensive and they are usually light enough to be carried easily all day by anyone unfamiliar with handling guns. The disadvantages, to my mind, are equally important. Lightness in any weapon can lead to uncomfortable recoil when the gun is used with anything heavier than the standard load, and this can be equally off-putting to an adult novice as to a child. The lack of second shot, a handicap discussed earlier, needs no repetition, but in all aspects of game and wildfowl shooting it is quite a serious disadvantage.

The third category involves the single-shot shotgun as a specialist gun. The 10 bore by Harrington and Richardson is a good example of this kind of weapon, being a heavy magnum single shot 10 bore for those special shots at extreme range against duck or geese. The other specialist single shot guns are produced to cater for

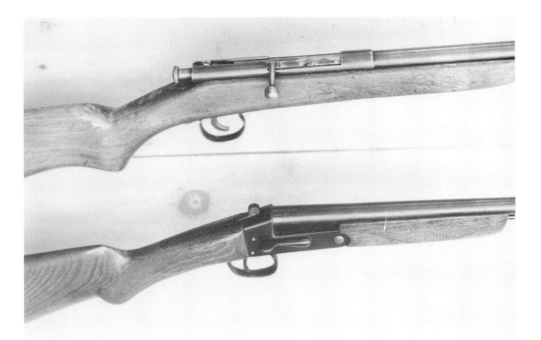

Figure 5.1   A bolt action and a semi-hammerless side lever .410 shotgun of English and Spanish origin

the American clay pigeon sport of single-barrel trap-shooting. These guns really are the exception to the general rule of single-barrel weapons, in that they are hand-made to the very highest standards of precision, craftsmanship, and artistry. Browning and Ithaca both produce hand-made single-barrel 'trap-guns'; but pride of place must surely go to the gun built to this format by Purdey. In keeping with their quality they are also heavy and expensive, being designed to absorb recoil and prevent the trapshooter being badly punished for firing hundreds of cartridges in the course of a day's competition.

The great diversity of designs one finds in the single-shot weapons that are currently in production, of course indicates that they are used in a variety of ways. Very many keen sportsmen find space in their gunracks, among their double-barrel and repeating weapons, for the odd single-shot gun. These guns are reserved for 'fun' days such as shooting rats around a haystack or walking the hedges for rabbit or pigeon, occasions when the shooting is at its most informal. Having said at the start of this chapter that the single-shot weapon is the least popular, let me now qualify the statement by adding 'for serious or formal shooting': an upland game shooter in American would be horrified at the prospect of swapping his beloved auto or pump for a single-shot, just as an English rough shooter would consider himself very out of place if he was not using his familiar double. Nevertheless, for informal shooting the single barrel is without equal. It has, over the years, established for itself a number of roles within the world of shotgun shooting and its popularity as the 'first choice' weapon for these purposes is not likely to change in the foreseeable future.

DESIGN

The great majority of single-shot shotguns conform to one basic design. They are made as a 'break-open' gun much in the same way as a conventional double-barrel. Like the double gun, most of these singles are opened by means of a top lever, but there is a greater incidence of variation from this in the single-barrel design. The side lever opening mechanism is quite often seen, particularly in the small calibre guns made in Southern Europe, and a variety of underlevers are also used by different manufacturers.

Three shotguns which compete for the same section of the market can highlight this. The Russian Baikal single shotgun is opened by a lever incorporated into the trigger guard which is pulled upwards into the action. In contrast to this, the Ithaca model 66 'supersingle' is opened by an underlever which is similar to the famous Winchester rifles. Another variation on the underlever comes from the Italian Mavi factory and marketed in Britain by B.S.A. and in North America by Galef, under the name 'Companion'. In this design the underlever takes the form of another 'trigger' set in front of the trigger guard, and operating this lever like a trigger opens the gun.

HAMMERS

Although some double-barrel hammer guns are still being made the vast majority of contemporary double guns have 'hammerless' actions. This is not so with the comparable single-barrel guns. Many, like the Russian Baikal and the Italian Mavi already mentioned, are indeed classed as hammerless guns, but there are also a variety of semi-hammerless and hammer guns on the market. The semi-hammerless action describes a mechanism in which the 'hammer' is partly concealed or protected within the action body. Often, only a small knurled spur protrudes because, like the true hammer gun, the weapon is cocked manually. In Europe this type of weapon is represented by the AYA Cosmos from Spain, and North American examples come from a wide range of manufacturers, such as Cooey (Canada), Winchester (Mod 37) and Savage-Stevens (Mod 94 C). Technically speaking, many single weapons described as hammer guns are really semi-hammerless, and contemporary models that are true hammer guns are rare. Nevertheless, some south European manufacturers do produce a small number of guns of this type, in which the hammers are actually on the outside of the action, but very few ever reach the open market.

Trap Guns

The most expensive and best quality single barrel guns, the specialist trap guns, are also built to this drop down design. These, however, conform more closely to the 'boxlock' action of the conventional double gun, but the Purdey Trap gun is made as a true sidelock shotgun. These weapons are bored to throw tightly choked patterns and a great amount of time is spent on regulating the bore of the barrel in

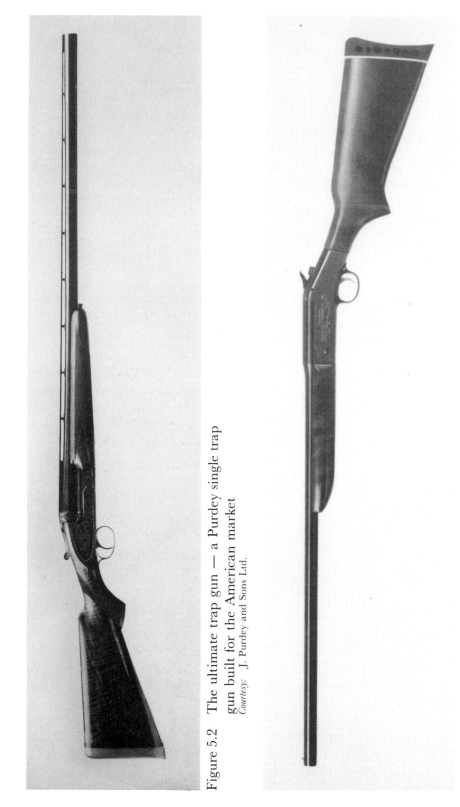

Figure 5.2 The ultimate trap gun — a Purdey single trap gun built for the American market

Courtesy: J. Purdey and Sons Ltd.

Figure 5.3 Guns for the novice — Harrington and Richardson Greenwing (Model 490) typical of the American design of simple 'boys' gun

Courtesy: Harrington and Richardson Co.

order to achieve this. These really are luxury weapons, and most examples can boast of the very best craftsmanship and the very highest quality of materials in their make-up.

Another similarity between these and the conventional double is that they are all, with the exception of the Lutjic series of trap guns, top lever opening shotguns. In this type of weapon can be seen examples of high class workmanship from many parts of the world, all competing for a share in the North American trap shooting scene. SKB of Japan, Franchi of Italy, Purdey of England and Ithaca of the USA all produce top quality weapons that compete against each other in the hands of America's best trap shooters.

Bolt Action

Two other single-shot designs take their ancestry from the world of military rifles. The first of these, bolt action shotguns, have been made for some time and, although the majority are either clip or tube-fed repeaters, a substantial number of single shot weapons are also made.

Although many 12 bore bolt-actioned single shot weapons were made in the past, nowadays the only true examples tend to be small gauge shotguns. Indeed the most popular gauge for the bolt action single shot is the .410, and a good example of this type of weapon was made by Webley and Scott. This firm, among others, also produced bolt action single-shot versions in the .360 or 9 mm Flobert calibre, and this can be classified as the smallest type of true shotgun in recent production. Also available on the current market is the 'converted' weapon. These are military weapons which have their magazines sealed and barrels bored out to .410 calibre. Thus, while retaining all the appearances of a military weapon they are, in fact, single-shot bolt action shotguns. In Britain the Lee-Enfield .303 is the weapon most usually converted in this way, but other examples exist in other parts of the world.

Martini Action

Finally, we come to one shotgun where the design stems from an earlier British military rifle: the Greener G.P. This is now manufactured by W.C. Scott and has a falling block Martini action based on the old .577 Martini-Henry military rifle. The great beauty of this action, in which the barrel is fixed and the breech exposed for loading by the breech block tilting downwards, is that it is immensely strong, durable, and rather heavier than many other types of action. Opening the breech is achieved by pulling the underlever downwards and experienced G.P. users can attain a fairly high rate of fire with their weapons, as reloading is a simple operation. Although the Martini action is a very old fashioned design, the Greener G.P. shotgun, which is made only in 12 bore and 16 bore, still remains a very popular weapon among single-shot enthusiasts.

Figure 5.4   Martini Action Greener 'G.P.' shotgun (top) and a top lever semi-
hammerless Brazilian shotgun — both in 12 bore

Because of its history, which reaches further back than any other type of shotgun,
the great diversity of successful designs currently in production, and the wide range
of uses to which the weapon can be put, the single-shot shotgun is an important type
of gun in its own right. Of course the design does possess certain disadvantages, but
then so does any other type of weapon. What does seem unfortunate is that the
inherent disadvantages in the single-shot gun have been rather overplayed by
adherents of the double and multi-shot weapons, but even they often derive great
pleasure in using single-shot guns on their informal, or fun days.

Whatever people may think of these uncomplicated weapons they are certainly a
well established type of gun for a variety of shooting and are likely to remain so for
as long as shotgun sport exists.

Figure 5.5   Many side–lever Singles like these .410s were built in the 'twenties and 'thirties and are still in use now.

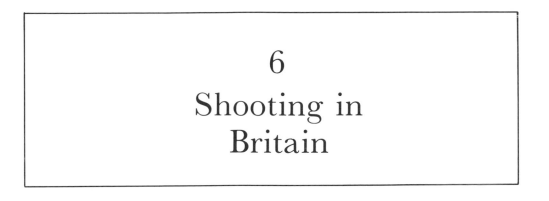

6
Shooting in
Britain

Figure 6.0   Grouse shooting in August. Shooting driven grouse is the cream of
British shooting.

Courtesy: John Marchington

Shooting in Britain

In terms of area the British Isles cover a very small portion of the earth's surface, and within these islands there is not a particularly wide range of physical conditions. The climate is equable, having a more or less evenly distributed rainfall throughout the year, and the overall range of temperatures is not very great. Under the influence of the warm waters of the North Atlantic Drift and the prevailing south-westerly winds, summers are warm and winters are generally mild. When we consider the actual land surface, here again there is no particularly great range of conditions. With the highest mountains barely scraping 4000 feet (1219 m) above sea level and two thirds of the land lying below 400 feet (122 m), the uniformity of the landscape and climate certainly do not seem conducive to providing a good range in the variety of shooting sports.

Yet this is not the case. Due, to a great extent, to Britain's long sporting heritage, the fact that this country played such a leading role in the development of sporting shooting, and also to its being in the forefront of the development of game management and conservation, Britain offers a rich and varied range of shooting opportunities. From the broad, flat coastal salt-marshes, through the green and fertile lowland farms, to the high heather and pine moorlands, this little country offers some of the finest shotgun shooting available anywhere in the world. The variety the country offers can be divided into four main categories, which relate generally to the variety of habitats and the species of game birds and animals each habitat can hold. In addition, a considerable amount of vermin shooting is carried out, that is, shooting such species as woodpigeon and rabbits, across a wide range of habitats, and this type of shooting is sufficiently important to warrant a category on its own. The four divisions I have made, then, are upland game shooting, lowland game shooting, wildfowling, and vermin shooting.

UPLAND GAME SHOOTING

In Britain, the term 'upland' usually refers to land from about 800 feet (244 m) to around 2000 feet (610 m) above sea level. At the lower end of this zone the landscape is slowly changing from enclosed pastures and small plots of arable land to rather more open moorland of heather, gorse and rough grass. In most parts of Britain the 800 foot (244 m) contour seems to coincide roughly with the 'tree line', where the native vegetation of broad-leaved, deciduous woodland gives way to

Figure 6.1   Approximate distribution of Red Grouse

hazel and willow thickets and low, windswept rowan trees. Most woodland above this line tends to take the form of man-made plantations of conifers, these being the only type of trees which can, through its rapid growth rate, return an economically profitable yield from such acid and peaty soil.

Within this zone, on the open moorland and on the periphery of the coniferous plantations, live the two most important of the upland game birds, the red grouse and the black grouse or blackgame. Of all the game birds of the British Isles, the red grouse is the most celebrated. The 'glorious twelfth' of August, the opening day of the grouse shooting season, never passes without some sort of press coverage, while the opening day for wildfowling, partridge and pheasant pass without comment. Rightly or wrongly, a day 'on the moors' grouse shooting is considered to be the ultimate in game shooting that Britain can offer.

Red Grouse

As a species, the red grouse is a bird unique to Britain, its nearest relative being the willow grouse of Europe, and it occupies a position in the moorland ecology which is not contested by any other species. It is very much a bird of the open moorlands, as its food needs are supplied by such plants as ling, crowberry and cranberry; all plants which occur on this kind of habitat, and the only times when the bird descends to lower farmland is when it is driven to do so by heavy snowfalls on the moors. This game bird is found, in small numbers, on the moorlands of south-west England, particularly Exmoor and Dartmoor, in rather greater numbers on the moorlands of central and north Wales, and on most of the open moorlands of the Pennines and Cumbria in England, and the upland areas of Scotland, where, through careful moorland management, the greatest numbers occur.

As a sporting bird, few who have shot grouse will claim that they have an equal. The dramatic, explosive flush of a grouse covey, the bird's incredible acceleration, and its very rapid contour-hugging flight make it an exceedingly difficult bird to kill. Add to this the fact that, after the breeding season, the birds gather in family parties or coveys, of up to twenty or so birds, and at times several of these coveys may 'pack' together so that the grouse shooter is presented with large numbers of relatively small targets hurtling across the moorland at an electrifying speed, and we can begin to understand the sort of challenge this sport presents.

There are two main methods of grouse shooting and these take the form of walked-up shooting and driven grouse shooting. In the former, the birds are walked-up and flushed, using either spaniels, setters or pointers to locate the birds on the ground. A 'gun' participating in a walked-up grouse shoot must be prepared to walk many miles for a relatively light bag, and must be equipped to face any foul weather the moorland has to offer. As the season wears on, the grouse will be flushed progressively further from the gun, so that rapid shouldering of the weapon and 'snap' shooting are an essential facet of the sport. Therefore, clothing as light as the weather conditions allow should be worn, and the shoulders should be kept free of any encumbrances, such as straps for game and cartridge bags. A cartridge belt with game carriers slung from it is the ideal solution, as it keeps the

Figure 6.2   The Red Grouse — a species unique to British moorland
Courtesy: The Game Conservancy

upper part of the body free to swing the gun on to what will be very rapidly disappearing targets!

As I stated previously in this book, choice of weapon is a very personal matter, but in my own opinion, the type of gun I would select for walked-up grouse would be one which was not too much of a burden to carry, that shouldered and pointed easily, and gave an instant choice of an open and a tight choke for shooting at a variety of flushing ranges. My own preference would be for a side-by-side 12 bore weighing around $6\frac{1}{2}$ pounds (2.95 kg), bored quarter choke in one barrel and full choke in the other.

In the old days, shooting driven grouse was very much the prerogative of the social elite. One was extremely fortunate if one was invited to shoot grouse, but times have changed and nowadays driven grouse shooting is more or less open to those who can afford the appropriate shoot fee. Rising costs, the increase in the general level of taxation and other factors led the shoot owners to introduce the 'paying guest' system on what were once exclusive shoots. This has brought the sport, which above all others is identified as a very British institution, within the reach of many shooters who are prepared to organize their finances in order to afford a day or two 'on the moors'.

Each driven shoot varies in the way in which it is financed and organised, but there are a number of aspects which are common to all. Most shoots are so designed that the birds are driven towards a line of turf butts in which the guns are placed. The grouse can come at the guns in ones and twos or in great packs, and this highlights the need for very quick reactions and rapid shooting and reloading. Birds are shot either in front, as they approach the butt or 'behind', after they have passed, and it is customary for the grouse shooter at such a venue to use a pair of guns. Compared with walked-up shooting, birds are normally shot at rather closer ranges, so the guns are often open bored. The degree of boring varies with individual taste; I know of one regular grouse shooter who has both his guns bored true cylinder in all barrels, and another who has his No. 1 gun, which he uses for shooting in front, bored both one-quarter choke and his No. 2 gun, for taking the birds behind, bored half and full choke!

It is on the grouse moors on these driven days that one most often sees pairs of 'best' double sidelock ejector 12 bore game guns, and as the shooting is at relatively close range, the 16 and 20 bore game guns are more often seen than in other types of shooting. To assist in rapid loading, a loader is usually provided by the host to keep the shooter supplied with a loaded weapon when the going gets hot. Skilled grouse shooters can, therefore, kill two grouse in front, swap guns with his loader and kill another two from the same covey behind.

Whenever grouse shooting in Britain is discussed, it is the red grouse that is taken as being the main quarry species, as this makes up the vast majority of the total upland game bag. The bird that is unique to Britain has caused a style of shooting to develop which is also uniquely British — the driven grouse shoot.

Figure 6.3   Walked up grouse shooting in the Scottish Highlands involves walking long distances in the course of a day's shooting
Courtesy: John Marchington

Black Grouse

Of the other three British upland game bird species — the black grouse, ptarmigan, and capercaillie — it is the black grouse which constitutes the second most important quarry species. The cock bird, known as the 'black cock', is considerably larger than the red grouse, but the female or grey hen almost equals it in size and weight. The range of this bird is similar to that of the red grouse, but as its habitat is considerably more specialised, being a bird of the hazel and willow scrub on the edges of upland coniferous forests, it is nowhere as numerous as its open moorland cousin.

Consequently, it seldom occurs in numbers great enough to warrant a specific 'black grouse' shoot, but the bird often forms an added attraction on a moorland shoot when a 'black grouse' drive may be incorporated into an otherwise exclusively 'red grouse day'. At other times, it is hunted by walking–up over dogs or by a line of walking guns, and when flushed from the confines of a birch or hazel thicket the bird offers a rapidly accelerating and difficult target. It is a very strong flier, usually at a height greater than the red grouse, and its flight is generally interspersed with long high-speed glides on down-curved wings.

In terms of gun and clothing, the same can be used on black grouse as is used for walked–up red grouse, and the skills and endurance of the shooter is tested as much by walking a mile of dense hazel scrub as walking three miles on open moorland.

Ptarmigan

Both ptarmigan and capercaillie occur only in Scotland, but their habitats are totally different. The ptarmigan takes over when the red grouse reaches its upper limit of around 2000 feet (610 m) and this severely restricts this bird to the upper slopes of the Scottish Highlands, where it has its stronghold in the Grampian Mountains. This species is the only member of the grouse family that can survive practically any extreme of weather that occurs on the high slopes and, indeed, is superbly adapted to these rugged conditions. In order to maintain its protective camouflage against the eyes of the golden eagle, fox or other predator, its winter plumage is completely white except for its black tail feathers. In summer, however, the only white it retains is on its wings, as the rest of the plumage becomes mottled greys and browns, in order to render the bird inconspicuous against the scattered clumps of heather, moss and bare rock which is its natural habitat.

With its rather restricted distribution, and being a bird confined to the more remote slopes of upland Scotland, the shooting of this species is carried out on a very limited scale. It is really a sport for the fit and the lucky: fit, because much of the day will be spent climbing to the zone inhabited by the ptarmigan, carrying gun, ammunition, and all weather clothing. Conditions in these comparatively low Scottish peaks can deteriorate with fatal rapidity and many walkers have met their deaths in these areas through being ill-equipped. In addition, ptarmigan are invariably walked-up, and many miles of walking and climbing will be undertaken during the day's ptarmigan shooting. The shooter must be lucky, because, with such a restricted habitat, few landowners are in a position to offer a day's ptarmigan shooting, and you have to be extremely fortunate to be invited.

As far as weapons are concerned, the type of gun described for walked-up grouse will also serve here. For those that have walked-up ptarmigan, there is one popular myth that they will quickly dismiss. It has often been said that shooting the bird is easy because they are relatively tame and will allow close approach. While it is true that they quickly become accustomed to man close to such areas as the ski lifts in the Cairngorms above Aviemore, where they are hunted they provide testing as well as exhausting sport. When shooting on loose rock scree after a climb of about 2500 feet (625 m), carrying all your equipment and food, the odds are stacked very much in favour of the bird!

Capercaillie

The last of the upland game birds, the capercaillie, is also the largest. The cock 'caper' can measure 3 feet (91 cm) from beak to tail and weigh anything up to 12 pounds (5.44 kg). It is no wonder it has been nicknamed 'the European turkey'. It was thought that this bird became extinct through forest clearance over much of North-East Scotland at the end of the 18th century, but birds were reintroduced into Perthshire in the late 1830's. Since then this strictly forest dwelling giant of the grouse family has reflected the general re-afforestation in many parts of the Scottish Highlands, by the steady increase in its distribution range. Its primary habitat is the pine forest which contains trees of differing ages, and although like other grouse, it is ground nesting, it spends much of its life among the branches of its native woodland.

Although it was at one time an under-rated game bird, shooting capercaillie as a sport is certainly now becoming more popular. Unlike other members of its family, this bird appears to have a lazy, slow and silent flight which gives the shooter the mistaken impression that it is an easy target. What he does not often realise until too late, is that the bird's great size belies its actual speed, and far from being easy targets these birds are most often missed by shooting behind. Birds are usually shot by driving them towards the guns, and many estates are now in the position of being able to offer driven days to let. So, like grouse shooting the sport is available to anyone who is prepared to pay the required fee.

Birds are killed at somewhat longer ranges than other driven birds, so the gun should bear a reasonable amount of choke in order to maintain a killing pattern with the larger shot that tends to be used. A 12 bore game gun, bored one-quarter and three-quarters choke would usually be combined with cartridges loaded with number five or even number four shot.

LOWLAND GAME

By way of contrast, the main population concentrations of the three important lowland game species — pheasant, grey and red-legged partridge — occur on the rich, low arable land of southern and eastern England. From the rolling scenery of the chalk downlands of Wiltshire, Hampshire and Berkshire to the low flat and intensively cultivated fields of the fenlands of South Lincolnshire, these three species have, by and large, maintained wild populations which are augmented annually by large scale breeding. Because the landscape and land-use provides the ideal habitat, these are the prime lowland game-shooting areas.

This, however, is a very general statement as there are many fine, well maintained and productive lowland game shooting areas as far west as Cornwall and as far north as Northern Scotland, but it is only in the south and east that the physical conditions come close to the ideal for the wild breeding of these birds. This has not always been so. Up to and around ten years ago the grey, or common, partridge population was showing a steady decline as farmers, particularly on the flat arable lands of East Anglia and Lincolnshire, uprooted hedges and used insecticides widely on their lands. Thankfully, those days have all but gone and a far more enlightened approach to the role of game management in farming has halted the decline. Even more recently, there has been a revival of interest in large scale rearing of both partridge breeds on shoots which at one time reared pheasants only. This can only bode well for the future of lowland game shooting.

Partridge

Of the three species the only true native bird is the grey partridge. Even with this species so many birds and eggs have been imported from time to time from continental Europe, that it is also called the Hungarian partridge. It is a bird of the open grassland or chalk downland and it also thrives on arable land upon which a

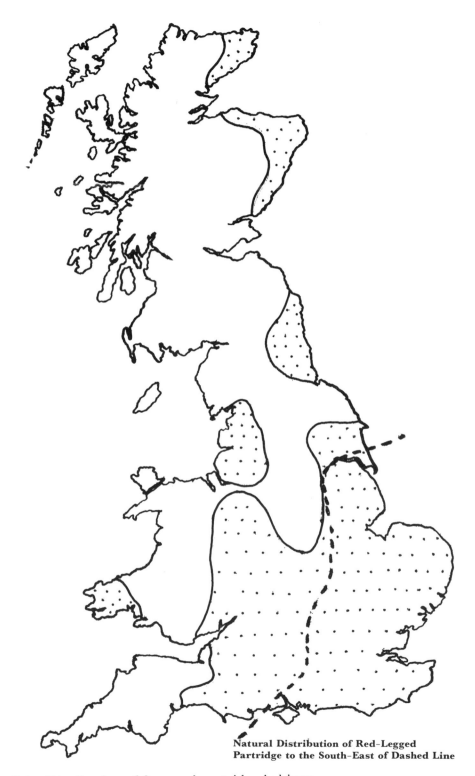

**Natural Distribution of Red-Legged
Partridge to the South-East of Dashed Line**

Figure 6.4   Distribution of favoured partridge habitats

variety of crops are grown. This provides the bird with a year round source of food
and shelter, but it also needs patches of rough ground, such as hedges, for its nesting
sites. Of the three birds, it is the most susceptible to wet weather and its numbers
fluctuate widely from year to year. As a game bird, it matches the grouse for its
explosive acceleration and sustained high-speed flight, but as with the other
lowland partridge, it does not have the endurance or the stamina of the grouse
species, and it is quickly tired by 'over-driving'.

The red-legged or French partridge, as its name suggests, was first introduced
into Britain from France about 200 years ago. Since then, it has spread its wild
breeding range throughout the area described and, because there is very little
competition between it and the grey partridge, both species live happily alongside
each other. For its habitat it tends to favour more sheltered ground and heavier
cover, and although it is a strong flyer, it prefers to hide from danger and is more
difficult to flush. The bird is generally thought to have less endurance than the grey
partridge and quickly becomes exhausted after two or three flushes.

Pheasant

With the population of both partridge species in a constant state of flux, the
pheasant must be considered the prime lowland quarry species. It has all the
attributes to make it so. When flushed it gains height rapidly and has a very fast and
strong flight. It breeds well in the wild, where it is more resistant to poor weather
than the partridge species, and it is the easiest game bird to rear under incubators
and broody hens. On a properly managed shoot they have less tendency to stray

Figure 6.5   The Grey Partridge — can withstand more severe winters than the
             red-legged partridge
             Courtesy: John Marchington

than the red-legged partridge, and of course, weighing up to $3\frac{1}{2}$ pounds (1.49 kg), they make a sizable and excellent meal. The Romans, during their occupation, are said to have introduced the bird to Britain but this wild stock was augmented by further introductions throughout the 18th and 19th centures, and the present-day stock is the result of the interbreeding of the various introduced races.

The bird's favourite habitat is one of mixed arable farmland and deciduous woodland, where it can feed on a wide variety of both animal and vegetable food sources. It is, however, also at home on coastal marshes and on the edges of lowland coniferous plantations and it is this ability to adapt to different environments that makes it such an important game bird to most lowland shooters.

The shooting of lowland game birds can be divided into two main forms. One method, known as 'rough shooting', will be described in detail later in this chapter; the other method is by driving the birds to the guns, and is known as 'driven shooting'. By the end of the 19th century, most of the large sporting estates had ceased striving for record bags on each shoot, and drives were being planned in order to present the most difficult and, therefore, sporting targets. At the same time two other factors were bringing about a change in the general sporting scene. The rising costs of rearing the stock and keepering the estate prompted — on these lowland estates as on the grouse moors — the 'paying guest' system, and this has now become the norm rather than the exception. The other factor was that shooting in the 20th century became the recreation of a much wider section of society who, not owning their own land, joined together in groups to rent shooting rights, employ part-time keepers, rear and release pheasants, and enjoy many days' sport. The shooting syndicate had evolved.

The Driven Shoot

It is by joining one of these syndicates that most shooters are introduced to driven game shooting, but as with most things in life, you get what you pay for. The least expensive are organised on 'rough shoot' lines, and the most costly usually provide plenty of high quality driven birds. On the driven shoots, the shooters (or guns) form only a small portion of the number of people involved, as the gamekeeper will have organised a team of beaters and specialist dog handlers for both flushing the birds and picking up the slain. Depending on the terrain and the stock of game, shoots are organised as partridge days, pheasant days, or mixed days, and at the end of the season there is usually a cocks only day, when no hen pheasant are shot. Although most shooting syndicates have a waiting list of shooters wishing to join, there are often occasions when a day may be 'bought' and the non-syndicated shooter can enjoy fine sport.

Only on the best shoots does one now see pairs of 'best' guns in action, and in these more egalitarian times the standard lowland game weapon is a good quality side-by-side or over-and-under ejector gun, bored about improved cylinder in one barrel and around half choke in the other. With this sort of gun the shooter can deal with a covey of partridge skimming over the low hedge on one stand and high curling pheasant on another with equal ease, providing of course, he has the skill to do so!

Figure 6.6   Most driven pheasant shoots attempt to present high and sporting
birds
Courtesy: John Marchington

The reader may have noticed that, so far, the double-barrel gun has been described, in one form or another, as the ideal weapon for both upland and lowland game shooting in Britain. This type of weapon, according to most British sportsmen, is the epitome of traditional 'good taste', and they look upon the single-barrel repeater guns with grave suspicion and mistrust. However unfounded these feelings may be, these American style weapons, while not actually barred, are positively discouraged on a great many shoots.

Before passing on to wildfowling, mention must be made of the 'secondary' game species one is likely to encounter on many shoots. Where the shoot includes marshes, or water meadows and woodland, **snipe** and **woodcock** may occur, but the numbers and distribution of these birds is dependent on the weather conditions. Only on a few occasions will the average shoot hold sufficient of these species to organise a special 'snipe' or 'woodcock' day. **Hares** and **rabbits** make up the 'ground' game of a shoot and, while the rabbit seldom occurs in enough numbers to organise days against them, many syndicates hold a hare drive after the game season has ended. These are often affairs where the beaters and other friends get their chance to shoot, and up to twenty-five guns assemble to cover the land in two 'teams'. These alternately act as standing guns and 'beaters' and often one hundred hares are killed by the end of the day. This is an effective way of controlling hare populations and gives the syndicate a means of thanking its beaters and helpers for the hard, and often cold, work they put in throughout the season.

WILDFOWLING

Due to the intensive breeding of lowland game bird species, and the careful management of the upland game bird habitats, it could be said that game shooting has become an artificial sport. Wildfowling, as practised on the foreshores of Britain, must be regarded as a truly wild one. Compared to all the forms of game shooting, shooting waterfowl in their natural environment is a solitary sport. The conditions in which a wildfowler may find himself may vary from September afternoons waiting for the odd duck on an inland flight pond to lying in freezing mud on a bleak ice-packed estuary in mid-January. His quarry include five species of geese, fifteen duck, and eleven species of waders, the hen-footed waterfowl. Often his shooting is carried out in rough weather and in poor visibility, so he must be able to recognise them quickly and be able to differentiate between those he can shoot and those that have legal protection. Poor light has never been a valid reason for shooting a protected or rare species.

All in all, the wildfowler must be far more aware of his surroundings than any other type of sportsman.

Basically, wildfowling can be divided into two main categories, and these are based on whether the birds are sought inland or on the coast. Even within these categories, considerable variations are possible, so that the sport of wildfowling probably offers the sportsman more variety than any other shooting sport. In addition to this, it is generally far more freely available and therefore attracts more participants than the other shooting sports.

Figure 6.7   The wildfowler is the 'loner' among Britain's shotgun users
Courtesy: John Marchington

Inland Duck

Inland wildfowling consists of intercepting, or seeking, duck or geese on their inland habitats. Any surface water has the ability to attract various species of duck, from the large natural lakes and man-made reservoirs, large and small rivers, flooded fen, gravel-beds, and watermeadow to artificially created flight ponds built for this specific purpose. Either the birds are shot by walking-up, a practice most common on rivers and small ponds, or they are shot as they flight to or from their feeding grounds in the early morning or late evening. In the latter case birds are enticed to establish a regular flight path to and from the chosen water by scattering corn along the water margins, and decoys are sometimes used in order to draw duck to the waiting gun. Eventhough this may seem a trifle artificial, the birds are usually truly wild-bred and wary. Shooting in the half light of dawn or dusk at these ghostly and swiftly moving targets can be both exciting and extremely testing. Walking up a river on a frosty November morning for the odd mallard or teal can be equally rewarding, and many of my favourite boyhood memories stem from such occasions in the Teifi Valley in Wales.

There is certainly more flexibility in the choice of weapon for inland duck shooting than in the various forms of game shooting. Any type of weapon you feel comfortable with can be used, and I see no reason why this should not be an auto loading, pump or bolt action shotgun. Whatever your choice of weapon may be, the bore should not be fully choked, as the average distance at which most inland duck are shot seems to be between 35 to 40 yards (32-37 m). Half choke would provide sufficient pattern density to cover all species adequately at these ranges. My own ideal choice would be for a $2\frac{3}{4}$ inch (70 mm) chambered 12 bore general purpose double, throwing one half choke and one quarter choke pattern.

The quarry species one would expect to shoot varies with location and the type of water. Wide shallow floodwater attracts the surface feeding ducks such as mallard, teal, pintail, shoveller and, in some cases, wigeon, while the deeper and longer established lakes and reservoirs would hold the diving ducks, such as pochard and tufted duck.

In a few areas **inland goose** shooting is possible, the quarry either being the introduced Canada goose, or the wild migratory grey geese, such as pinkfooted or white fronted geese. The grey geese species can be decoyed to their feeding fields or intercepted on their flight lines from their coastal roosting to inland feeding ground, but the localities where this is possible are few and far between. Canada geese are not a really successful sporting proposition in this country as these introduced birds often become far tamer than their transatlantic cousins, but in some cases they are wild and strong fliers and give sportsmen a chance to bag what is now Britain's largest goose.

Coastal Wildfowling

Coastal wildfowling is somewhat different. The foreshore in the depths of winter is no place for the unobservant, foolhardy, or the unprepared. In no other shooting sport does the participant expose himself to such a wide variety of dangers and yet gain such a degree of inner satisfaction from pitting himself against the elements

Figure 6.8   A 'fowler with gun and dog on the wide and lonely expanse of
salt marsh
Courtesy: John Marchington

and his wild quarry and, sometimes, succeeding. Awareness and preparation are the key words. The wildfowler must be aware of the dangers of being cut off by a flooding tide, suffering from the effects of exposure and being trapped in soft estuary mud, which are all part and parcel of this pursuit, and his preparations should be made to minimize these risks. A novice in this field must seek local knowledge and guidance before venturing forth. He must know which are the danger areas, as well as the flight lines and movement patterns of his quarry species. He must be able to recognise his targets in dim light by wing beats, shape and calls, and he must equip himself for any eventuality. He will often find himself alone in wild and desolate places where his own personal survival comes before considerations of the sport he can enjoy. This sport is probably closer to our idea of 'Man the hunter' than any other shooting situation.

As with inland shooting, quarry species vary with different parts of Britain's coast, but probably the bulk of the bag is composed of the surface feeding duck already mentioned, except that wigeon now form a substantial part of the bag. Pinkfoot and whitefronted geese are the shore shooter's largest quarry and greylags also feature in some areas. Of the 'hen-footed' waterfowl, curlew, snipe, whimbrel and redshank offer very different shooting and excellent eating, and the fast flying golden plover often form a welcome addition.

The foreshore was once the domain of the big gun. In the inter-war years mighty four and eight bores roared at great flocks of duck and geese, but alas, those days have gone and with them the big guns. Nowadays one only sees a big gun in the hands of a die-hard traditionalist who is prepared to pay the very high price for ammunition. Similarly, the high cost of cartridges keeps the 10 bore very much a minority weapon, except where large numbers of geese occur, but very often they are used by novices questing for longer range and heavier loads. The really ubiquitous wildfowling gun is the 3 inch (75 mm) magnum 12 bore. More often than not they are strongly built, inexpensive doubles, but repeaters are also used by a fair number of foreshore gunners. Standard loads range from $1\frac{1}{4}$ to $1\frac{1}{2}$ ounces (35–43 g) of number four or five shot, although larger sizes are used for geese and smaller shot and lighter loads for waders. Experienced gunners will quite rightly maintain that heavy loads are intended to maintain good pattern density with large shot at normal 'magnum' ranges of up to 50 yards (46 m), rather than to extend the gun's range any further. The novice shooter, in this area where range judging is difficult anyway, will always be easily identified by his attempting long range shots which, in the long run, are both unsporting as they often wound rather than kill, and counter-productive in that they needlessly scare and disturb the wildfowl.

The **National Association for Shooting and Conservation** (Formerly WAGBI) is the controlling body for this sport and anyone, however remotely connected with 'fowling', should take it upon themselves to become a member. Indeed, he will not be allowed on many areas of foreshores unless he has enrolled. This association in addition strives for the continuance of all manners of shotgun sport, takes active steps to ensure the preservation of prime wildfowl habitat and has inaugurated the large scale breeding and release of many species of duck throughout the British Isles.

ROUGH SHOOTING

Having discussed some spects of the main forms of game and wildfowl shooting, let me describe what is now probably the most popular kind of informal shooting — the rough shoot. Much of the enjoyment derived from this kind of shooting stems from the sheer pleasure of being in the open air on an autumn or winter's day, the variety of game that may be brought to bag, and the appreciation of watching a good gundog at work. On an average lowland rough shoot, the end of the day may show pheasant, partridge, duck, woodcock, snipe and hare among the overall bag, but all these would appear in small numbers. Here is shooting, not for the ultimate size of the bag, but for variety and the unexpected.

Most rough shoots rear game birds on a small scale, take steps to encourage wild breeding stock and feed any water margins to attract waterfowl. Occasionally small drives are organised, but most game is shot walked-up, and the informality and good company on a day's rough shooting make it, for me, one of the most enjoyable of shooting sports. Access to a days rough shooting is within the reach of most people, and the cost of joining a rough shooting syndicate is far lower than for a driven shoot. As with other forms of 'social' as opposed to 'solitary' game shooting, the weapon that is considered to be ideal is the double 12 bore game gun of the type suggested for walked-up grouse.

VERMIN SHOOTING

The last of my four main categories may be loosely termed 'pest control' or 'vermin shooting'. In its broadest sense it encompasses the controlling of all birds and animals that predate on game birds, and aiding the farmer in crop protection by the shooting of rabbits and pigeon. The first of these, the control of carrion crows, magpies, jays and ground predators, such as foxes, stoats and weasels, is one of the main preoccupations of the gamekeeper. While the .410 is considered to be the ideal anti-vermin weapon, much vermin is also shot by newcomers to the shooting sports using a variety of weapons from air rifles to 12 bores. While guns are used for winged vermin, modern and efficient trapping methods are far more effective methods of controlling ground vermin, and the shotgun takes on a very secondary role.

The same can be said of rabbit control. Since the advent of myxomatosis, rabbits seldom occur in numbers great enough to merit organised rabbit shoots, but the animal often figures in the bag on rough shoots and other sporting lets. One of the more popular methods of rabbiting is by using ferrets to either bolt them from their holes so that the gun is presented with a shot, or to drive the rabbits into a net where they can be quickly despatched.

Woodpigeon

To the shotgun user, the most important aspect of pest control is woodpigeon shooting. So great is the crop damage that flocks of these birds generate, that in many parts of the country shooters have formed 'crop protection groups' in order to coordinate the shooting of this species. The woodpigeon, Britain's largest and wariest dove, is a strong and agile flier and is thus considered a sporting bird as well as an agricultural pest. The pigeon shooter can, therefore, feel happy in the knowledge that in shooting these birds he is not only enjoying fine sport but is also doing the farmer a good turn.

Two main methods of shooting pigeon account for the great majority of the birds brought to hand. Decoying the bird to a waiting gun concealed in a suitable food crop field is a practice which with skill, experience and luck, can account for a great number of birds. The art of setting out the decoys, concealment and shooting from relatively cramped positions all have to be learned, sometimes by instruction but more often by trial and error, and pigeon shooting in this way keeps many a game shooter or wildfowler in practice during the close season.

The other kind of pigeon shooting is known as roost shooting, as the participant intercepts the birds moving to or from the roosting woods. In the warm days of summer the birds may offer many easy shots, but on a blustery November evening birds returning to roost will be flying high and fast, often curling and side-slipping through the wind. On such occasions not even driven high pheasant could offer more testing targets.

The 'general purpose' shotgun is an ideal weapon for pigeon shooting, but many decoy experts go for open bored skeet guns as the birds over decoys are frequently shot at closer range. The pigeon has a very loose plumage and, because even one shotgun pellet can cause it to lose a lot of feather, it has gained a reputation for being difficult to kill. This reputation is not really well founded, as examination of plucked birds will reveal that just one or two small shot can easily penetrate the plumage and kill the bird.

In most parts of Britain, pigeon shooting is there for the asking. Providing the shooter respects the game and follows the 'country code' most farmers are only too pleased to have the pigeons thinned off their crops or from their woods. In many ways this is the ideal way of introducing a newcomer to shotgun sport as, to be successful he must quickly learn the rudiments of field craft, concealment and shooting accuracy, all skills he will need as he progresses to rough or game shooting and wildfowling. Add to this the fact that the bird makes excellent eating, and one begins to realise why the 'wily woodpigeon' is classed as an important standby quarry species.

Throughout the length and breadth of the British Isles, the variety and quality of shooting is what we have come to expect from a group of islands so well steeped in the sporting tradition. From the packs of grouse driving over the butts in Britain's uplands on the twelfth of August to a wild and stormy January dawn on some windswept estuary, the variety of sport available in Britain is far greater than any other comparable area of land in the world. More important, most of the shooting described in this chapter is available not only to British shooters, but on a daily basis to any visiting sportsmen who are prepared to make arrangements in advance. Far from the traditional image of shotgun shooting being the pastime of Britain's gentry, much of the best quality shooting is now available to anyone who wishes to participate and who is prepared to pay a fee for his enjoyment.

Figure 6.9   The author with grey partridge on his syndicate's rough shoot
Courtesy: Arthur Bierschenk

7

Shooting In Europe

Figure 7.0   A pair or trio of guns, a case of cartridges, and as many red legged Partridge as you can shoot
Courtesy: Spanish National Tourist Office

Shooting in Europe

To any sportsman wishing to shoot game in Europe, the prospects can, at first sight, be quite disheartening. Many European countries seem very reluctant to allow visiting shooters access to any form of shooting, others operate on an invitation only system whereby permission to shoot will only be granted on production of a written invitation from a landowner in the host country, and the general impression the sportsman may be left with is that the European continent is very much a closed shop. When various National Tourist offices are approached on shooting matters, their lack of information on shooting facilities highlights the fact that the touring sportsman is still poorly catered for on the Continent; indeed, it appears that whatever shooting opportunities do exist, European sportsmen are keeping them very much for themselves. This is not, however, really a true picture.

From the sunny shores of the Mediterranean to the high tundra of Northern Scandinavia there are a great many areas where a variety of game can be hunted with shotguns. Not only does a wide selection of available game and wildfowl exist, but the traditional shooting methods vary from country to country and this adds a new dimension to the sport.

THE QUARRY

The fauna of continental Europe includes a wide variety of game species which are the traditional quarry of the shotgun user. These species can be divided into three broad categories: game birds, wildfowl and ground game. The number and variety of these species a shooter can expect to encounter varies with locality and environment.

Game Birds

Game birds can be sub-divided into two groups which are defined in terms of their distribution and favoured habitat. Such birds as the capercaillie, black grouse, willow grouse, hazel hen and ptarmigan can be called the northern game birds. Their distribution is more confined to the northern regions of Europe where natural vegetation of coniferous forest and tundra predominates; this only occurs as isolated pockets in the mountainous areas in the more southerly regions of the

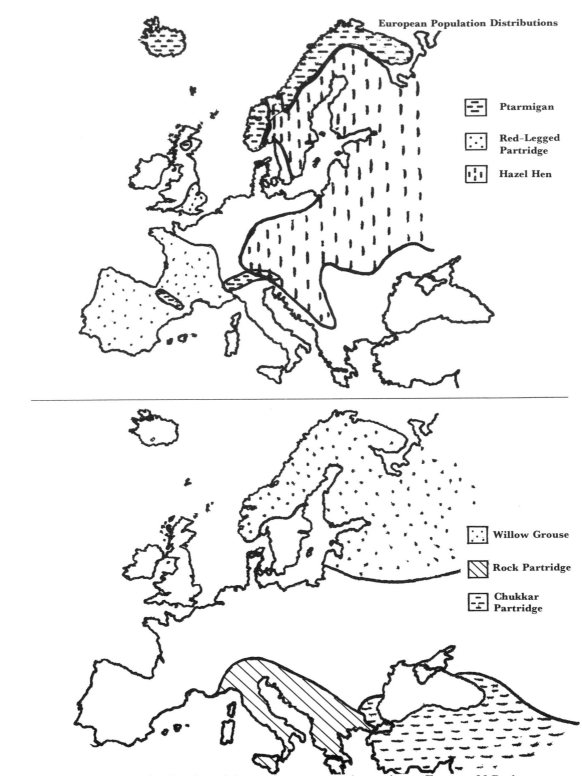

Figure 7.1   Distribution of the main game species native to Europe. N.B. the grey partridge is omitted as it occurs over most of this area

continent. These northern species each occupy a certain kind of habitat within the natural vegetation, and therefore seldom compete with each other for food or breeding areas. The fact that they do occupy different habitats has however led to a number of different styles of shooting, some of which will be covered in greater detail when I describe the kind of sport available in the Scandinavian area.

The southern game birds include the pheasant, red-legged, chukkar, and rock partridge, with the grey partridge maintaining a sort of intermediate position between the northern and southern species. All these birds, at the northern extent of their individual population ranges, are lowland species which have adapted to a wide variety of farmland environments. As we progress southwards, however, the same species of bird may take to scrub-covered hillsides and generally more arid areas, and this forms their main habitat in the countries that border the Mediterranean Sea.

Wildfowl

There are about thirty species of duck and ten species of geese that occur in the wild state in Europe, and many of these are classified as prime shotgun quarry. From the salt pans or 'salinas' of the Mediterranean area to the lake and forest scenery of Finland and the Baltic Shield, wildfowling is an important facet of the shooting sport in many European countries, and each area holds its own quota of resident and, in season, migratory waterfowl. Unlike the North American continent, Europe does not have a number of clearly defined migratory routes or

Figure 7.2   Red-legged Partridge breed so well in Spain that no rearing programmes are necessary

Courtesy: John Marchington

'flyways' that are more or less rigidly followed by a variety of waterfowl species. The closest we come to it is the Northern Siberia to Western Europe coastal route. The more northerly breeding waterfowl tend to have, instead, a general and dispersed spread southwards during the autumn, and birds breeding in eastern Europe tend to move westwards at the same time. In the winter months, therefore, huge concentrations can gather on the western coastline of Europe and here, in the past, they have been over-exploited to such an extent that there are now vast areas along the coast that are strictly controlled wildfowl reserves.

Ground Game

Although it can already be seen that Europe offers a wider variety of quarry species than Britain, in terms of both game birds and waterfowl, it is the diversity and abundance of ground game that really highlights this. As well as the deer species that occur in both areas, Europe also has its populations of elk, wolf, lynx, reindeer, bear and wild boar. With such a variety of 'big game' it is understandable that many European countries think of rifle shooting as the primary shooting sport and classify shotgun shooting as second best, an attitude that certainly generates much argument and discussion. Even though rifle shooting predominates in most areas, the shotgun user can still find a good variety of ground game that are considered as suitable shotgun quarry in many parts of the Continent.

Of these, the wild boar is the largest and the most dangerous of the 'shotgun' species. This animal, which is widely distributed over most of Europe, is usually

Figure 7.3   Distribution of the European wild boar — dotted area indicates the probable extent of the wild boar in recent years (maximum)

hunted with dogs or by driving. In either case the sudden appearance of a large, angry and potentially very dangerous animal at close quarters can certainly make for exciting sport. Other species of shotgun quarry include the arctic hare, brown hare and the rabbit, and these figure mostly in mixed bag shooting although, as in Britain, each species sometimes occurs in such numbers that they are controlled by special organised shooting.

EUROPEAN SHOOTING REGIONS

It would be impossible, within the confines of this chapter, to describe in detail the type of shooting that is available in each of the European countries and, indeed, if I did much of the information would be repetitive. What I have done, therefore, is to select specific countries or areas in order to describe the typical environment and the game it holds and the type of shotgun sport that has been created, on a broader basis. I have consequently divided the continent of Europe into three regions which have distinctive climate, natural vegetation and available sport. The first of these is called the Mediterranean region and it includes Spain, Italy, Yugoslavia and the other lands on the coast of that sea. The second is the Northern region, which encompasses all of Fenno-Scandinavia, and the third is the central region, which ranges from the Irish Republic, in the west, to the borders of Russia in the east. Each of these three regions is described in general terms before discussing, for each, some specific shotgun sports which should give the reader a clearer idea of the shooting that is available.

SOUTHERN EUROPE

The Mediterranean region takes in the lands of the hot, dry summers which are so beloved of the coastal resort bound holiday makers. Even the winters are mild and the rains which fall predominantly in that season replenish the landscape, parched by the summer sun. These are also the lands of the olive and citrus groves and vineyards, but much of the terrain is rocky, steeply sloping and scrub covered. Away from the coast there are the upland plateaus, the sierras and, in the north and east of this region, these rise even further to the High Pyrennees, Alps and Dinaric Alps.

Game Birds

Of the game birds, the red-legged partridge is the most important in the western section of the region, its population distribution covering north-west Italy, most of Southern France and all of the Iberian peninsula. Further east it is replaced by two species, the rock partridge occupying the lightly wooded slopes of Italy and the lands east of the Adriatic, while the Chukkar covers the same range but prefers drier and rougher habitat. In some parts of this region pheasant, either wild or reared, also thrive, but really this species is better suited to the cooler climates and

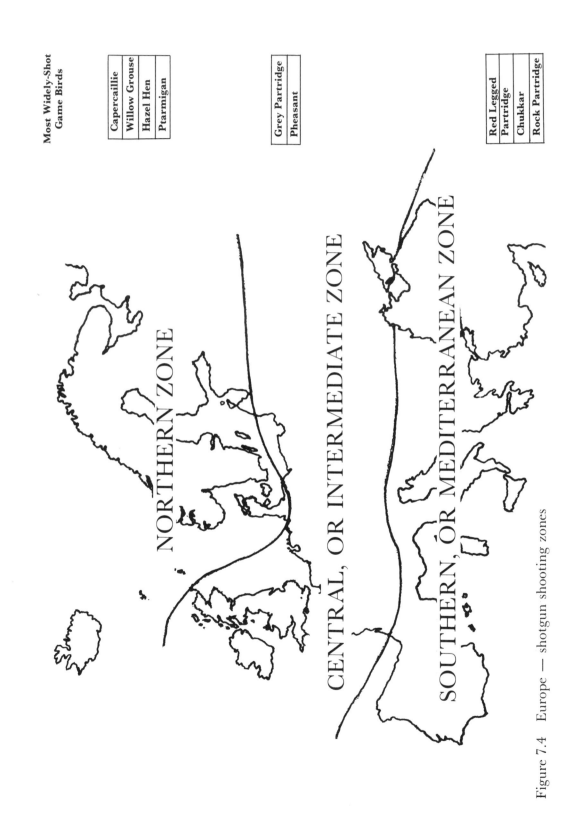

Most Widely-Shot Game Birds

| Capercaillie |
| Willow Grouse |
| Hazel Hen |
| Ptarmigan |

| Grey Partridge |
| Pheasant |

| Red Legged Partridge |
| Chukkar |
| Rock Partridge |

NORTHERN ZONE

CENTRAL, OR INTERMEDIATE ZONE

SOUTHERN, OR MEDITERRANEAN ZONE

Figure 7.4 Europe — shotgun shooting zones

greener landscapes north of the Pyrennees and Alps. In these mountains capercaillie and ptarmigan also can be found, although geographically these localities are far south of their respective population strongholds, and to the east of the region these two forest and mountain species are joined by the hazel-hen and the black grouse. These essentially northern species are confined to rather small areas of mountain habitat in this southern part of Europe and, therefore, although each is hunted, they cannot really be considered as the major sporting species that they are further north. The three species of partridge, in their respective areas, are undoubtedly the most important game birds of the region.

Wildfowl

The wintering ranges of most species of migratory European geese do not reach into this region, so, but for a very few exceptions, the wildfowler in southern Europe is essentially a duck shooter. The Mediterranean climate being what it is, there are few extensive wetland areas along the shores of the sea, and the lack of much surface water is one of the features which characterise this region. Nevertheless, where large rivers empty out into the sea, or where there are extensive salt evaporation lakes, wildfowl often gather in great numbers. One has only to think of the Po valley in Northern Italy, the Carmague in the South of France and Las Marismas on the Guadalquivir in southern Spain to realise that this region contains wetlands of world importance. As for shootable species, most of the common northern European duck are also well represented in this region. Surface feeding ducks such as mallard, pintail, shoveller and gadwall all contribute to the region's sport, as do the common diving duck, such as pochard and tufted duck. In addition there are species not usually found in other parts of Europe: red-crested pochard, ferruginous duck, Garganey, and white-headed duck add variety to the fauna of the wetlands.

Ground Game

The brown hare is found over the whole region, but the rabbit is only found west of Italy although, as in every other region, its numbers have been considerably reduced by myxomatosis. Changes in farming methods over the last thirty or so years have not really affected these two species, but the gradual loss of suitable habitat has caused the distribution of the wild boar within the region to undergo a general contraction. This large animal now occurs in the remoter parts of Yugoslavia, in isolated pockets in the Appenines of Italy, but is widely distributed over much of Spain and Portugal.

Italy

Italy, long steeped in a tradition of fine artistic gunmaking and a variety of shooting sports, tends to keep the shooting for itself. From all the accounts I have listened to or read, much of the country is 'overshot' and game of every description is nowhere plentiful, except on the many well-keepered estates. Even so, one is left with the general impression that the wildlife of that country has been over-exploited and any moves to provide sporting facilities for visitors would only serve to increase pressure on an already strained resource.

Yugoslavia

Yugoslavia has recently begun to open its borders to the travelling shooter. At the present moment much of the activity is centred around the wild boar drives in the north eastern part of the country, but there may well be a broadening of the facilities if the Yugoslavian authorities find that these early ventures are successful. Certainly the country seems to have great sporting potential, both in the variety of game that may be available and by virtue of the fact that, being less industrialised and less densely populated, it has a larger proportion of remote and unspoilt country which, with proper management could produce very good sport.

Although the southern quarter of France falls into this Mediterranean region it will be referred to later in the chapter. At the time of writing, Albania and Greece appear to be closed to the shotgun shooter, which leaves us with the two countries of the Iberian peninsula, Portugal and Spain.

Iberian Peninsula — Spain

In general sporting terms both these countries can be considered together, but it is Spain that has become justifiably world-famous for its shooting facilities and, in particular, for its partridge shooting.

Hunting the red-legged partridge takes up 90 per cent of the total time spent on either big or small game shooting in Spain. It is not unnatural, therefore, that the sport evolved many different shooting methods which are bound by their own traditional tactics. These methods range from the 'al salto', where one man hunts and shoots birds over a pointer, through 'manos encontradas' when a group of shooters divide into two teams to alternately act as standing guns and beaters, to the large scale shoot known as 'el ojeo'. It is for this last method, the formal driven partridge shoot, that Spain has won an international reputation.

So ideal is the terrain and climate and so abundant is the year round supply of food, that very many of the large sporting estates can boast bags of up to 25,000 partridge per season, without ever needing to implement any artificial rearing programme. These estates let the shooting on a weekly basis to parties of between ten and fourteen guns, and shooting normally takes place over five days. As the whole operation is geared to catering for the foreign shooter, nothing is left to chance and everything is included in the cost of the week. On the Casa Tojo estate, for instance, the accent is on creating a combination of relaxation and excitement. The guests are catered for, in terms of accommodation and food, to a very high standard and, apart from the actual drives, the week is spent at a relaxing and leisurely pace.

A typical shooting day starts shortly after dawn when, having breakfasted, the guns meet their loaders and board the coach which takes them to the estate. Soon the party transfers to cross-country vehicles, which takes them to the first drives of the day. An hour or so later the shooter is at his first stand, drawn by lots, accompanied by his loader or 'cargador' and his picker-up or 'secretario'. Shooting on this scale has to be carried out using a pair of guns, as in the course of the day the shooter may expect to fire about 150 cartridges. While his guns are being unpacked and loaded, the beaters, up to forty of them, are lining out perhaps over a mile away to walk the first drive. One of the characteristics of the Spanish red-legged partridge is the ability both to fly and to change direction very quickly. These birds, in the three drives before lunch and the two after, offer a wide variety of very challenging shots against the magnificent back-drop of the scrub covered and rugged Spanish landscape.

It is not unusual to average a bag of over one hundred birds for each drive, and occasions when the daily bag is over six hundred birds are reasonably common, but ultimately this depends not on the number of birds seen, but on the skill of the shooting party. To my mind this is shooting in the luxury class, comparable to the best grouse moors of Britain but with the added bonus that even in January, the sun usually shines warmly enough for shirt sleeves and relaxed outdoor lunches. The abundance of truly wild birds which present a variety of exciting, difficult and often hectic shooting makes shooting partridge in Spain the cream of what the Mediterranean region has to offer.

Northern Europe

By way of contrast, the high snow capped and fir clad mountains and the numerous lowland lakes of the northern region of Europe can offer shotgun sport which, though completely different, nevertheless can be just as enjoyable. This region covers the area known geologically as the Baltic Shield and the Scandinavian mountains. To the east the rocks that form the very foundation of the European continent have been exposed by the scouring of successive Ice Ages to form a low landscape of ice deposited ridge and ice carved hollow. A large proportion of Finland and lowland Sweden is the result of this action, which has created a woodland and lake scenery. To the south the great ice sheets washed out great quantities of sand, gravel and other debris in the melt-water, which covered much of western Denmark with dry and infertile deposits while, on the country's eastern side, boulder clays which generate heavier but more fertile soils, filled the ice hewn hollows. To the west, the remains of the vast range of mountains thrown up by the inexorable movement of the Eurasian and North American continents still remain as the high mountain backbone shared by Norway, on the west, and Sweden on the east. The west coast itself is the land of the fjord, those deep and steep-sided inlets that were created by the erosive action of glacier, now together add up to a vast area of relatively calm and sheltered water in an otherwise rugged, and in winter, inhospitable region. In winter, therefore, when snow and ice grips the mountain lakes and rivers, these sheltered waters become a haven for the thousands of displaced waterfowl.

Only in the extreme south of the region do forests of deciduous hardwoods thrive, but these broad-leaved woodlands are confined to the low and sheltered zones. As the land gains height they are quickly replaced by vast forests of conifer and these in

turn are only replaced in the far north and on the high mountain slopes by true
tundra vegetation. One characteristic of this Scandinavian coniferous forest,
however, is that as well as containing a variety of conifer species, it also has
substantial belts of willow, hazel and birch scrub. Far from being a region of one
type of habitat, therefore, the northern zone of Europe contains a variety of
environments which, in turn, cater for the food and shelter needs of the rich variety
of game species that can be found.

Game

In addition to the 'northern game birds' mentioned earlier in the chapter, these
forests are also the home of much larger game. Roe and Red deer occur in most
parts of Norway and Sweden and there are also substantial populations of moose
(elk) and wild reindeer. Other big game that can be hunted include bear, wolf,
wolverine and lynx, and with such a variety of large ground species, it is
understandable that the shooting scene of these northern countries should be
dominated by rifle sports. Nevertheless, there is legislation in Norway for instance,
that prevents most species of small game being shot with anything but shotguns,
and this affords the shotgun user rights which otherwise might have been eroded by
the rifle's priority.

The lowland gamebirds, pheasant and partridge, are only to be found to the
south of the northern region, although with only a few exceptions, they are
nowhere plentiful. Broadly speaking, the northern limit of their natural range
roughly coincides with the 'southern boundary' of this region and climatic
conditions are such that wild breeding birds, grey partridge in particular, have a
very precarious existence. Pheasant, as stated in chapter six, tend to be more hardy
and therefore wild stock of this species breed reasonably successfully in Denmark,
southern Sweden and around Oslo in Norway. Indeed, some landowners on the
Danish islands run pheasant shoots on very similar lines to those found in Britain,
supplementing the natural wild stock with rearing and releasing programmes.

The most widespread, but not necessarily the most common, upland gamebird is
the black grouse, as its distribution covers all of the northern region except for the
high tundra in the extreme north. The rocky scrubland with which the coniferous
forest is interspersed is its favoured habitat, and even in a country as intensively
farmed as Denmark, sufficient of this sort of environment remains for the black
grouse still to be considered as an important game species.

The capercaillie and the willow grouse also have a widespread range, although
the former is considered absent from both Denmark and south Sweden. The
capercaillie's natural preference for mature pine forest in hilly or mountainous
areas preclude it from lowland Denmark, but it is the most prized of the shotgun
quarry in Norway where it is estimated that around ten thousand are shot each
season. Without doubt, however, it is the willow grouse which is the major shotgun
game species in this region. This bird, which is now regarded as conspecific with the
red grouse of Britain, is a bird of the heather moors and willow, birch, and juniper
scrub of the Scandinavian coniferous forests. As such, it is an uncommon bird in the
south of the region, but its range extends northwards well into the arctic circle.

Figure 7.5   The Capercaillie is a highly prized game bird of the northern forests

Courtesy: The Game Conservancy

The remaining two birds of the grouse family occupy contrasting habitats. As in Britain, the ptarmigan is really a bird of the tundra, occupying the high mountain slopes in the south of its Scandinavian range and colonising progressively lower land towards the north. The Hazel Hen, on the other hand, is a bird of the low undulating mixed woodlands of the south and east cost of Sweden, Finland and the limited lowlands of Norway. Both these birds occupy environments unsuited to the needs of the other, more widespread game birds, so that throughout the region there is always a quarry game species in any given habitat.

Woodcock shooting is a more widespread sport in this region than in any other part of Europe. The estimated autumnal population of Norway alone is around the 200,000 mark, and around 10,000 are shot in that country per season. With the abundance of surface water, wildfowling is also of great importance with all the major northern species of duck and geese being hunted both on the inland lakes and along the coast. Seasons vary between each country, but wildfowling generally stops before the really hard weather in January and February takes its own natural toll on the birds that have not migrated further south.

Denmark

With this wide range of quarry species, the shotgun user can find a great variety of sport in Europe's northern region. Denmark, with its wide, low arable landscape holding more lowland game than the other countries, is rather untypical of the rest of the region. Shooting rights in this country belong to the landowners, so access to shooting is normally by invitation only. Pheasant and partridge are normally shot by driving and the shoot's organisation tends to be more formal than an equivalent British shoot. This, in itself, cannot be considered a bad thing, as the formality stems from a great awareness of safety among Danish sportsmen.

Wildfowling, on inland flight ponds and on the coasts of Denmark's many islands, can be of the highest quality. Positioned as it is on one of the prime European waterfowl migration routes, the numbers and variety of species sometimes encountered can be exhilerating. Though rabbits do not exist on mainland Denmark, hares are plentiful and hare shoots are organised frequently. In all, Denmark offers a good variety of high quality sport, but the limiting factor for the visiting sportsman is whether or not he can obtain a landowner's permission, or invitation, to shoot.

Norway

To the north of Denmark, Norway is, in my opinion, far more accessible and offers a wider variety of game bird species than any other country in the northern region. As in Denmark, the shooting rights usually belong to the landowner, but often he rents these rights out to interested parties or hotels. Consequently, many local shooting groups and hotels are able to offer the visiting sportsman access to shooting. As stated earlier, shotguns only are used for the pursuit of all gamebird and waterfowl species and a variety of shooting methods are used. Capercaillie are hunted early in the season over pointers, but later in the year, when the birds are more often flushed from trees, this becomes difficult! About 20,000 black grouse are shot each season by the same method, but the main sport in practically every region of Norway is the pursuit, in a similar manner, of the willow grouse. So abundant is this species that an estimated 500,000 are shot each season without affecting the population status of the bird. Towards the south of Norway, hazel hen are also hunted, and these small, fast flying birds have the same sort of attraction, and present as difficult a target, as walked-up woodcock.

Weapons and Shoots

The double barrel shotgun, be it side-by-side or over-and-under, is the most popular and commonly used weapon in the northern region. Indeed legislation in Norway restricts automatic loading shotguns to a two shot capacity. Generally, these countries tend to minimise the paperwork, and formalities concerning a visitor importing his weapons into the region for sporting purposes, and this certainly helps the shooting holiday get off to a good start.

A driven shoot is a rare occurrence in Scandinavia, where the local sportsmen derive greatest pleasure from either hunting alone with one dog, or at most, shooting in small parties using a team of pointers or retrievers. Walked-up shooting is the norm and, although no heavy bags are made, the variety and the unexpected nature of the sport amid the breathtaking mountain scenery in parts of these northern countries are the source of a great many unforgettable memories for any sportsman who has hunted there.

THE CENTRAL REGION

Between the two regions already described lies the broad 'Central Region' of the European continent. Stretching as it does from the Atlantic coast of the Irish Republic in the west to the Russian frontier in the east, and from the low flat reclaimed polders of the Netherlands to the high Alps on its southern boundary, it probably has the greatest range of environments of all the three regions. It is only natural to assume that this great range of different environments also produces the greatest variety of available shooting, but this natural variety is added to, here more than in either of the other two regions, by the many different methods of shooting that have evolved in the different countries for the various species of shotgun game. However, the general rise in the affluence of Western Europe has been reflected in the increased pressure on the wildlife resources of the continent from hunters, photographers and other interested groups, which has resulted in a general contraction of the availability of shooting access for the travelling sportsman. What I have chosen to do, therefore, is to describe the sport that is available in two countries at opposite ends of the region and follow this with a more general description of the type of sport that may be made available to a visitor to the more central countries.

The Irish Republic

To the extreme west of this central region lies the Republic of Ireland. This country, which has undergone great social change since the beginning of the 20th century, now readily welcomes visitors, who approach the shotgun sport that the country offers with a degree of sportsmanship. This has not always been the case. In the early part of the century much of the country was bound up in large sporting estates which, like their English counterparts, were very well keepered, very exclusive or very expensive. The political changes since those days saw the division of these estates into small farms of around sixty acres each and the shooting rights passed to the owners of these holdings. Obviously this saw the end of the large scale game rearing, but to hasten the game stock decline, the doors were opened to shotgun users from the continent. The great majority of these continental visitors appeared to 'shoot anything that moved' and it tended to turn all the Irish sportsmen very firmly against the visitors. Through an enlightened approach by both Irish sportsmen and Government, however, to the field of game management and conservation Ireland is again in a position to offer a good range of shooting to the visitor, providing of course, he sticks to shooting the accepted game and wildfowl quarry species.

Although some driven shoots exist in Ireland, they are geared to cater for the tourist only, and are therefore as expensive as the best England can offer. The average visitor to Ireland must thus be prepared for a lot of walking, be able to enjoy working closely with dogs, and be satisfied with small bags (compared to driven shoots).

Pheasant is the main game bird, but cocks only are shot as hen birds are fully protected, and the main method of shooting is walking–up over pointers or setters. Although partridge and red grouse are found in Ireland, the generally moist climate does not suit the former, and the latter is only common in a few, rather restricted areas.

The Republic is a land of extensive peat bogs, and in this habitat snipe shooting is one of the most testing and popular sports the country can offer. Unusually, these areas are also the home of the blue or arctic hare, which in other parts of Europe only colonises the higher mountainous regions. Both inland and along the extensive coastline, wildfowling is of great importance, and Ireland holds wintering populations of most species of European duck and the Greenland sub–species of the whitefronted goose.

Again, as with most other European countries, there is no general restriction on calibre of shotgun, but the most popular type of gun has a double barrel construction. Automatic and repeating guns must be restricted to a three shot capacity, but apart from that, few restrictions apply. The 12 bore is the accepted normal calibre and cartridges for the other calibres may be difficult to obtain in some of the remoter areas of the Irish Republic.

Nevertheless, for any visitor who is prepared to walk for his sport and is happy to have about six or seven head of game or wildfowl to show for a day's shooting, The Republic of Ireland will not only offer them a great welcome, but will also provide them with some very enjoyable sport.

Figure 7.6   In Ireland, as elsewhere, the snipe is considered a very testing target for the shotgun user

Eastern Europe

The variety of sport that is available to visitors to the communist bloc countries on the eastern edge of the central region contrast markedly with the shooting in Ireland. Countries such as Poland, Czechoslovakia, and Hungary have only recently begun to exploit what is a vast potential market by providing a wide range of hunting facilities for the touring sportsman. For the shotgun user **Hungary**, for instance, offers a wide range of lowland game bird shooting, wildfowling and driven wild boar.

In all these types of sports, the actual cost can depend on the scale of organisation involved, and the number and quality of game shot. Pheasant shooting is arranged either for driven or walked–up days. Obviously, because more people are involved in a driven day, these are more expensive and are normally arranged for parties of ten guns or more. The scale of shooting on these days can be appreciated by the fact that the organiser can, in some areas, practically guarantee daily bags of over 800 birds.

Bag limits are decided before the shooter sets out on the day, and where this limit falls is dependent on how much the shooter or party is prepared to pay. Partridge shooting is generally a walked–up sport and very often they are included in a mixed walked–up shoot when pheasant, partridge and duck may be shot.

Wildfowling on the many Hungarian lakes takes three main forms. Walked–up shooting along the reed fringes of these waters is very popular; there are also areas where special reed hides accommodate a duck shooter, and shooting from a boat on open water can also be productive. Huge numbers of migratory duck and geese winter on the Hungarian plains, and, although the individual wildfowler is well catered for, facilities also exist for wildfowling parties of up to ten guns.

Hungary has quite substantial populations of hazel hen, black grouse and capercaillie, but these are not generally offered to the visiting sportsman, and the shooting of hares is severely restricted and in some seasons even prohibited.

One sport Hungary does offer, however, and perhaps the most exciting of all shotgun sports, is the shooting of driven wild boar. Here teams of dogs and beaters drive the boar towards the waiting guns, and the sudden appearance of an angry tusker as close quarters must be the best incentive to accurate shooting Europe can offer. Naturally, for this type of shooting, specialist ammunition is essential. Very large buckshot, ball or rifled slug loaded cartridges are generally used, but perhaps the most popular is the Rottweil Brenneke finned slug. As with all loads of this type, greater accuracy is obtained from open bored barrels and one of the specialist 'slug guns' from the American manufacturers would serve as a very effective wild boar gun.

As for the other forms of shotgun shooting, any type of shotgun may be used, but it is advisable to choose either 12, 16 or 20 bore as ammunition, for the other calibres may be difficult to obtain. Certainly the accent in Hungary is on providing the visiting sportsman with well organised shooting, and this can often lead to very enjoyable sport. In future very many more western shotgun users will be looking towards Eastern Europe for variety and exciting sport, two factors upon which Hungary's sporting reputation is based.

The countries that occupy the most central positions in this region, **France, Belgium, Holland** and **West Germany** also appear to be the most difficult in terms of sporting access for a visitor. Here, more than in any other part of Europe, the countries seem to wish to keep the shooting for themselves and to a large extent do not have any facilities for the visiting shotgun user. Yet it can hardly be said that these are non-sporting countries, the gunmakers of Liege, St. Etienne and Suhl had already established fine reputations before Manton appeared on the scene.

Generally, shooting access is by invitation only, although even a written invitation may not be the answer to all the problems associated with importing and using weapons in these countries. Perhaps it is unfortunate that France in particular has gained a poor sporting reputation through its treating a wide variety of birds, skylarks and thrushes included, as shotgun game. Nevertheless, many of its chateaux can produce driven pheasant and partridge to equal any in the world. Its Mediterranean, Atlantic and Channel coastlines also produce wildfowling of a high standard, but this is again marred by the French sportsman's apparent inability to distinguish common from rare species!

West Germany, on the other hand, boasts shooting sports that are so traditional as to appear regimented to the outsider. The larger game birds, such as the capercaillie and black grouse are only hunted during the breeding season and only the cock birds are shot. Other species of 'small game' are more conventionally hunted by walking-up or driving during the autumn and winter.

Usually on these driven shoots, a wide variety of game may be encountered, and this gave rise to a uniquely German weapon called the 'drilling' combination shotgun and rifle, and one such gun may have up to two shotgun barrels and two rifle barrels of different calibre. Though as a rifle it is not accurate at distances over 150 yards (137 m), most of the game is shot at close quarters and these weapons can cater for practically any contingency. A person so armed would therefore be able to shoot anything from wild boar to snipe at one loading and these guns are understandably very popular on driven shoots when their weight does not constitute a burden.

All shooting sports in Germany are carried out with considerable formality and any visitor lucky enough to be allowed to shoot must be very careful not to transgress any of the traditional customs, although of course this advice is applicable to any type of shooting in any country. The common sense rules of courtesy, sportsmanship and safety are, however, universal and will always be an appreciated quality in the visiting sportsman.

From the shooting I have described in this chapter the reader will, I hope be able to conclude that Europe, despite its being the smallest continent, can offer a considerable variety of challenging and exciting sport in a variety of climates and environments. Perhaps most important of all, this choice of shooting is not the prerogative of a privileged few, but is available to all who wish to allocate the necessary resources to enable them to participate. For these, I have included in the Appendix a list of addresses of the organisations and agencies which will help them plan their shooting holiday in Europe.

Figure 7.7   East European countries can offer opportunities to hunt Wild Boar.
Courtesy: Mavad, Budapest.

8

North American
Shotgunning

Figure 8.0   Upland game in thick cover requires a light quick–pointing auto for 'reflex shooting'.

Courtesy: Arthur Bierschenk

North American Shotgunning

The North American continent is a paradise for the shotgun user. No equivalent land area on the earth's surface can offer anywhere like the same variety of game species, the range of environments, and the positive accessibility for shooting sports that is available north of the Mexican border and south of the Arctic ocean. A glance at the natural vegetation map in any atlas will immediately show that the number of different types of natural habitat is far greater than exists on the European continent, and each of these natural habitats has evolved a group of indigenous game species. From the frozen wastes of the Arctic Tundra, through the forest and grassland regions to the burning deserts, at least eighteen major native species of the quail/grouse family can be encountered, which is well over double the European species count. Add to this the areas in which the pheasant, grey partridge, chukkar and french partridge have been introduced and one is confronted with the widest possible variety of 'hen-footed' game birds one could find in any two countries of the world.

During two seasons of the year huge numbers of waterfowl make their migrations which traverse the continent from north to south, flying to the south from their nesting grounds in late summer and early fall, and making the return trip in late winter and early spring. At their wintering grounds and along their migration routes they provide a rich variety of wildfowling sport, from coastal gunning much in the same manner as European coastal wildfowling, to calling in the odd duck to a prairie water-hole. Here again, the number of separate species is greater than is found in Europe, giving a correspondingly richer variety of sport.

Although the continent does not have an equivalent to the European woodpigeon, it does hold a number of species of dove which are also included in the list of quarry species that are available to the shotgun hunter in North America. While the vast majority of the animal or ground game species are considered to be 'rifle targets', one species of deer in particular, the white-tail, has caused the evolution of a specialised shotgun type which will be described in detail later — the slug gun.

Even from this brief introduction it will be perfectly obvious that it would not be possible to deal adequately with such a wide and rich variety of shotgun sport within just one chapter of this book — such a study would take many volumes! What I therefore propose to do is to subdivide shotgun shooting in North America on the basis of habitat rather than by region as I did in the previous chapter. I will

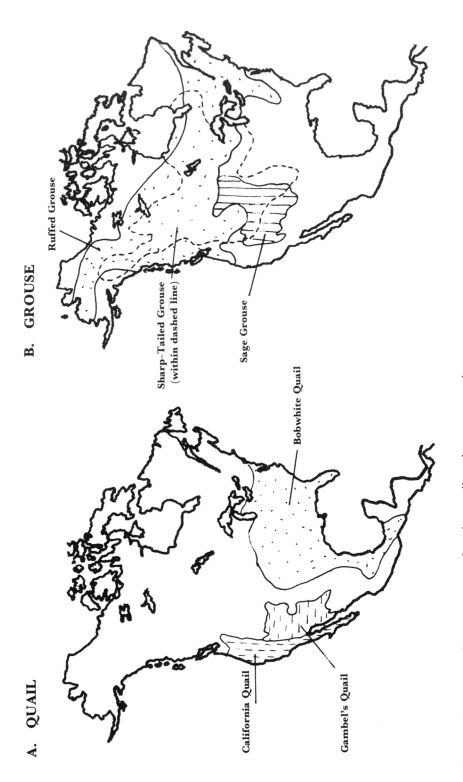

A. QUAIL

B. GROUSE

Ruffed Grouse

Sharp-Tailed Grouse
(within dashed line)

Sage Grouse

Bobwhite Quail

California Quail

Gambel's Quail

Figure 8.1   Approximate ranges of main quail and grouse species

describe the game birds of the woodland and forest as a separate group from those of the open prairies, scrub and desert, though there are many areas where the range of species in either category may overlap. I will then describe the waterfowl and the introduced gamebirds, ending with a brief description of the ground game for shotgunning sport. Categorisation like this is possible because, unlike the European land area which is subdivided into numerous small countries, each with their own hunting regulations and procedures, North American shooting comes under just two national governments. Admittedly, each state of the U.S.A. and province of Canada formulate their own seasons, and other hunting controls, but there is a unity and cooperative spirit over the whole continent that is lacking in Europe. Access to shooting grounds is generally very much easier than in the majority of countries in Europe, and it is therefore not surprising that old-world sportsmen, conservationists and naturalists look to the North American continent with envy.

GAMEBIRDS — UPLAND SHOOTING

To the outsider, gamebird shooting in North America seems to be divided into the two broad categories of upland shooting and waterfowl shooting, anything else being thought of as rather incidental to these two divisions. The term 'upland' here refers to all gamebird hunting carried out in areas away from waterfowl habitat, the birds themselves belonging to the *gallinaceous* family of quails, grouse, and turkey.

Species Available — Woodland Birds

Strictly speaking the true upland game birds are those of the mountain and high forest areas, although of course this must include the northern tundra and sub-arctic conifer forest areas as the same birds inhabit these as inhabit the mountains and forests further south. The true upland gamebirds would, therefore, include such species as the ruffed grouse, blue grouse, and spruce grouse — all birds of the conifer forest — all four species of ptarmigan, the mountain quail and, on slightly lower open woodland, the turkey. The wide range of species reflects the wide range of habitat within this category. In the far northern tundra the ptarmigan is the main grouse species, while in the broad belt of the coniferous forest further south and in the snow clad mountains of the Canadian Rockies, the willow, rock and white-tailed ptarmigan take over as the major quarry species. The lower, denser forest of pine, spruce and fir with an undergrowth of poplar and willow is the main habitat for the spruce and ruffed grouse. This is particularly true of the Canadian range of these species, because the further south one comes, the greater is the altitude at which their favoured habitat is found. The U.S. distribution of both spruce and ruffed grouse appear, therefore, to be centred on the mountain states of Idaho and Montana.

The blue grouse, another coniferous forest dwelling bird is more confined to the western mountains of the continent than the other two, with a range stretching from British Columbia and Yukon in the North to the Montana valleys as far south as California and New Mexico. This bird, the second largest of North America's grouse, can weigh up to 4 pounds (1.8 kg) and is also perhaps the least hunted because of its remote habitat. The largest of the quail family, the mountain quail, occupies a similar though more restricted range, being a bird of the west coast states, though Idaho is again the predominant area.

Hunting methods for these birds show a considerable variation according to the terrain, the weather, and the numbers of people and dogs involved. Success in hunting often depends on the amount of work done before the season begins, in locating areas containing a stock of birds, and getting to know their daily movements to and from feeding, resting and dusting areas. In comparison with such species as the bobwhite quail, relatively low numbers of these forest and mountain birds are shot during each season. This is probably because their particular habitat includes much of the wildest and remotest mountain areas of the continent. In some parts this results in the birds being rather tame, but once flushed, the flight of the mountain quail, and all grouse and ptarmigan species, is fast and exhilerating. They are all strong runners, and wounded birds usually require a dog to locate them and bring them to hand.

Perhaps the most popular shooting method is to hunt them over dogs — parties of two or more hunters with pointers or other flushing dogs working slowly through likely patches of cover in the hope of finding game. Hunters without dogs often organise drives similar to the European method, by which a section of woodland is blocked off and 'driven' by a group of hunters working towards some 'standing guns', who intercept the flushed birds.

Weapons

Unlike the gamebird shooter in Europe, who is rather hide bound by traditional taste in terms of the choice of the type of gun that can be used, the gamebird hunter in North America has much greater freedom in his selection of weapon. This then comes down to personal taste or preference, though it seems that the multi-shot weapon, be it an auto or repeater is by far the most popular. This is, perhaps, the most natural choice for such shooting in the remote mountain and forest areas. A rugged and dependable gun that can be field-stripped with the minimum of bother and few tools, is the ideal type of gun. It must be remembered, however, that a day's hunting often involves a great deal of walking, so one of the lightweight repeaters would be my choice. Short barrelled and fairly open bored, say modified choke, the gun would be easy enough to handle in thick brushwood to enable the user to come to terms with these fast flying and elusive gamebirds. Many arms manufacturers produce 'upland' double guns which are also very popular, probably due to the instant selection of two choke borings, but the type of shooting does mean that the guns used undergo a fair amount of rough treatment. Under such circumstances a repeater would, undoubtedly, prove the more popular gun.

Woodcock and Turkey

Two woodland game birds have not yet been properly mentioned. These are the woodcock and the wild turkey. These have not been included with the others in this group because their habitat, range and distribution make them birds of the south and east, rather than of the north and west. This does not mean, of course, that they are confined to the south and east, as some mid and western states can boast of large numbers of each species.

Like the forest grouse species, the woodcock is not as heavily shot as it might be, but the reason for this is different. It is a comparatively small gamebird and, therefore, considered by many hunters as not worth the cost of ammunition; it also inhabits very heavy cover which makes flushing and shooting difficult. Nevertheless, its flight makes it a testing target even to the most experienced hunter, as it rarely presents itself for a shot for more than a fraction of a second and its flight follows a highly erratic course. For this reason a lightweight gun bored improved cylinder is the type of weapon to use. I would even go for an open bored 20 bore in order to gain the advantage of lightness and quick pointability. Even though a light double gun has many advantages to commend it, a pump or auto for woodcock shooting in these circumstances is probably still the better choice.

The turkey is a rather special bird. Unlike most other gamebirds, this large bird of open woodlands is hunted in two seasons. The fall season is the time when most birds are shot, but the spring breeding season gives the turkey hunter the chance of bagging the large male birds in their peak breeding condition. Weighing up to 20 pounds (9 kg) or more, the wild turkey is North America's largest gamebird, but

1976 estimates in shaded states gave turkey populations of over 10,000 birds.

Figure 8.2   Distribution of wild turkey in the United States

Figure 8.3   The wild turkey is hunted in many parts of Central and
              Southern USA
Courtesy: P. Kaminski, Stagsden bird gardens

hunting methods often mean that they are killed at fairly close ranges, and large size shot is therefore not needed. Even so, it would, in my opinion, be unwise to shoot turkey with shot sizes smaller than five, or with any of the smaller gauge guns.

Most turkeys are hunted by following their calls and stealthy approach and in the spring season experienced hunters can call in the male birds by imitating the voice of the female bird. These shooting methods demand a great deal of patience and determination on the part of the hunter, who must count himself lucky if he gets in one or two shots per hunting trip. Here the double gun is often more the favoured weapon as its operation is generally more silent than any weapon with a sliding bolt. In a sport where silence and stealth is of paramount importance, the quietness of a shotgun's operation when being reloaded becomes a very significant factor.

Open Ground Birds

Among the species that can be categorised as the 'open ground' gamebirds, those birds that inhabit the farmland, open prairies and semi-arid areas of North America, we find the most frequently hunted and popular of all the continent's gamebirds, the bobwhite quail. This bird's distribution range is approximately centred on the mid-western states of Nebraska and Kansas, though they are plentiful in all states to the east of these (with the exception of the extreme north east) and in a number of states to the west. It is really a bird of the woodland and farmland margins, colonising the rough areas around the boundaries between these two environments, and it has adapted well to the changes that have taken place in farming methods in recent years, something which cannot be said for other gamebird species in this group. Though it is widely distributed this is a bird of central, southern and eastern America, and is replaced towards the west by a group of quail species which are often known collectively as 'western Quail'. These include the California quail, Scaled quail, Gambel's quail, and Mearn's quail. The grouse family is also represented in this open ground category by such species as the prairie chicken, the sharp-tailed grouse and the sage grouse, yet these are again birds of the mid to far west of the continent as they prefer the drier, high chapparal and sage brush country.

Three species of quail — Scaled, Gambel's and Mearn's — are predominantly birds of the arid south west. The first two of these have very similar ranges, with their population centred on New Mexico and Arizona, although both may be found as far north as Idaho and as far east as Oklahoma. Mearn's quail has an even more limited range, being really a Mexican bird whose range extends northwards into Arizona, New Mexico and Texas. For this reason it is sometimes referred to as the 'mexican bobwhite', Living in such arid areas, the availability of surface water is often the governing factor in their local distribution and here again, man's activity, in the form of land improvement and irrigation schemes, has allowed the birds to increase their range. In other areas their numbers depend on rainfall and the resultant vegetation growth so the hunter may find it very difficult to locate large numbers of birds in any one season.

The last of the important quail species, the California quail, is very much a bird of the west coast, as its population is centred on California, Oregon, and Washington though large numbers also exist in Nevada and Idaho. Like its cousins of the more arid areas, it is a bird fond of watercourses and rivers, hence its alternative name of valley quail. The vegetation of the intermontane valleys of the west coast states is very much more luxuriant than in the drier south and the bird has adapted its habits and diet to profit from the intensive farming towards the north and the irrigation and orchard farming towards the south.

Quail hunting methods vary according to the land cover, terrain and the habits of the individual species, but the most universally accepted method is to use a good flushing dog in order to get the birds to fly. All quail species are notorious for their initial reluctance to take to the wing, except when they gather in large coveys in late summer and early fall. At that time of the year, species such as the California quail may gather into coveys of 500 or more birds, and then they are not only difficult to approach but also are only too ready to flush. At other times all quail species are far more likely to run from approaching danger than to fly. Once a covey has been flushed, however, it is normal for the hunter to try to mark down the landing area of individual birds and to hunt these with the flushing dogs. The quail then tend to sit very tight, only flushing when the dog (or human) is within inches of the bird! In this situation the hunter needs a quick pointing shotgun as the speed of a flushed quail is quite startling. Their small size only adds to the impression that they are rocket propelled! It is often difficult for a lone hunter to get to grips with a covey because they will try to keep ahead by running, so the most successful hunting involves a number of hunters who can block off the ground escape routes

Figure 8.4   The bobwhite quail — to the visitor the bird symbolises North
American upland game shooting
Courtesy: P. Kaminski, Stagsden bird gardens

and force the birds to sit tight until flushed. Though the bobwhite and California quail live in generally hospitable areas, the hunter of the semi-desert quail can encounter additional difficulties when hunting their quarry. The natural vegetation areas, the low cover in which the quail can sit tight, includes cactus and thorn scrub which can and often does deter the most keen flushing dog. In such circumstances flushing the bird, and tracking down a winged bird, can be decidedly unpleasant. However in more open country, hunting these semi-desert quail is often an exhilerating sport.

If the quail species appear, with the exception of the bobwhite, to be birds of the south and west, then the 'open ground' grouse species may be termed birds of the centre and north of America, with their ranges extending into the prairies of Canada. Of the three species, the sharp tailed grouse is by far the most widespread. Its population is centred around Nebraska, the Dakotas and Montana, but the bird ranges extensively through the prairie provinces of Canada to as far north as Alaska, and separate sub-species or races of this bird extend the range to the Pacific coast in Washington and British Columbia in the west and to Pennsylvania and the Hudson Bay in the east and north-east. In one way the sharp-tail grouse resembles the bobwhite in that it is a bird of the marginal habitat of the open brush country between forests and open prairie. As such, its numbers can fluctuate quite markedly as a result of land improvement or forestry and lumbering. Large scale forest clearance increases its habitat and consequently its numbers, but as the forest regenerates, its numbers will decline again.

Nowadays the sage grouse has a far more restricted range than the sharp-tail, though at one time it was much more widespread. Being a bird of the open sage brush plains and the foothills of the Rockies, its distribution has contracted with the spread of stock grazing and the systematic destruction of its sage brush habitat. Nevertheless, it is still found in large numbers in Wyoming and its adjacent states, and the Pacific coast states also hold significant populations. In terms of weight it is second only to the turkey, the male bird weighing anything up to 8 pounds (3.6 kg). Being such large birds, they take off slowly when flushed, but their acceleration is so good that within 20 or so yards (18 m) of their take off they are travelling very fast. Their size often misleads the hunter into thinking that they are actually slower, and the sage grouse are most often missed behind. When the birds are fairly regularly hunted they have a tendency of flushing further from the gun and flying longer distances. So much so that it may be nearly impossible to mark down singles from a covey flush.

In order to give a 'knock down' blow to these large birds, a more heavily choked gun than one would use for quail is needed, the ideal choking being about improved modified (or three-quarter choke) and a larger shot size is needed for greater penetration. In this open country, the hunter may have to travel long distances in order to locate coveys, though the most favoured habitat appears to be sage basins less than a mile from water. A good flushing dog is always useful, as in any 'walked-up' game shooting, and one favoured method of hunting the sage grouse is for parties of hunters and dogs to line out and walk an area of sagebrush in line abreast. In this way a much larger area can be covered than is possible by one man and his dog.

Figure 8.5   The California quail is restricted to the western States where it is a
favourite game bird
Courtesy: P. Kaminski, Stagsden bird gardens

Of the three grouse species that inhabit the open spaces of the continent, the prairie chicken is by far the most restricted in range and the least common in overall numbers. Like the sage-grouse its once extensive range has been steadily eroded by the advance of arable farming and stock grazing, so that nowadays only six states of the U.S.A. allow the bird to be hunted at all. Even in these states, which can be considered as their population stronghold, they are found only in limited areas. South Dakota, Nebraska and Kansas can be taken as the states in which there is a good stock of birds, but they also occur in small numbers as far east as Michigan and west to Wyoming.

Hunting tactics for these birds change as the season progresses. Early in the season a good flushing dog can be employed as they lie well at this time, but as the season progresses they flush at increasing distances so that by the end of the season a dog can prove to be a serious handicap. Early season shooting calls for a fairly open bored gun, but by the close of the season there is a strong argument for using a full choke barrel and heavy shot in order to connect with the birds flushing far out.

Viewed overall, open ground gamebird shooting in North America can offer a wide contrast in environment, species and hunting method. From hunting the Gambel's quail in the burning semi-desert of Arizona, helped by a close flushing dog and using an open bored lightweight gun, to walking in line over a large area of high plain's sage brush in Montana, in the hope of finding a covey or two of sage grouse, the open lands of the continent can provide the hunter with some very enjoyable sport.

WILDFOWLING

Compared to upland gamebird shooting, most waterfowl hunting can be looked upon as a passive sport. In the former, the gamebirds are actually hunted and flushed by dog and man, in other words, hunter goes to the hunted, whereas in the latter, the hunter tends to wait for the hunted to come to him. Shooting is most usually carried out from some sort of concealing hide or blind; which is sited in an area that waterfowl are known to frequent. The sport of the waterfowler or wildfowler is therefore very much a waiting game, and he employs a variety of methods in order to persuade any quarry species in the locality to fly within his gunshot. The other big difference between the wildfowler and the upland hunter is that the former hunts birds that are mainly migratory.

Of the twenty-six or so species of duck and seven species of wild geese on this continent there are about thirteen types of duck and four of geese which are the North American waterfowler's prime quarry. In general terms, these birds breed towards the north of the continent and migrate during late summer and early fall to their wintering areas towards the south. The distances covered in these migration movements varies with each species, but the route taken on migration has been categorised into four distinct movement zones or flyways. These are:

1.   The Pacific — following the west coast from Alaska and the North West Territories to as far south as the Baja California and beyond.
2.   The Central — following the north-south trend of the Rocky Mountains and

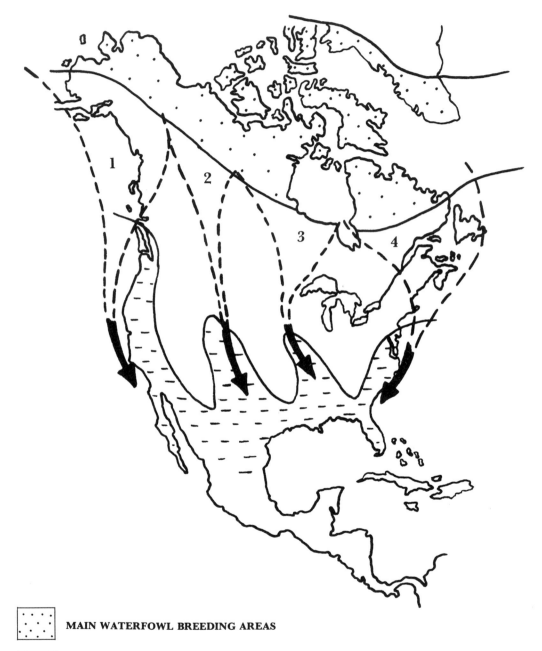

 MAIN WATERFOWL BREEDING AREAS

MAIN WATERFOWL WINTERING AREAS

Figure 8.6 Principal migratory routes of North American waterfowl; 1 Pacific;
2 Central; 3 Mississippi; 4 Atlantic.

High Plains that form the mountains' eastern shoulders.

3.   The Mississippi — following the course of this great river system from north to south.

4.   The Atlantic — following the east coast from Labrador and the Hudson Bay area in the north to Florida in the south.

The duck species can be further sub-divided according to their feeding habits into surface feeders (or puddle-ducks) and diving ducks; also their feeding methods often dictate the type of locality in which each species is found. Surface feeding birds have a preference for the reed-lined margins of ponds and lakes, with water depths of 2 feet (61 cm) at the most. They rely for their safety on their ability to lift off the water in one movement and gain height in a very steep and rapid climb. The diving ducks, on the other hand, favour open water which has a depth of about 10 to 15 feet (3–4.5 m). By staying in the open they have good warning of approaching predators. Take-off is accomplished after pattering along the surface, and their rate of climb is generally much less than that of the surface feeding ducks, although their flight is often more rapid.

Surface Feeding Ducks

Of the surface feeding duck species, the mallard is undoubtedly the most common and widespread, its range covering practically all areas of the continent. It is not, however, a common bird in the extreme north east of North America, its place being taken by the closely related black duck. The mottled duck, another close mallard relative, is found along the coastal marshes and swamps of the Gulf states and Florida. They are all large ducks, and all, apart from the colourful drake mallard, are an overall brown colour and are, therefore, often confused with the female mallard. Though these species occur in great numbers on certain favourable coastal areas, they are predominantly fresh water ducks with a preference for river-fed ponds and lakes.

The same can be said of the Gadwall, though this smaller duck, which to the inexperienced eye also appears similar to a female mallard, is nowhere really numerous. Its main migration tends to follow the Central and Mississippi Flyways and it is most abundant on the open water of the central plains and even further west. They are rather better divers than the other surface feeders, and their flight is light, buoyant, and rapid.

Pintails are often considerd the most elegant duck, and certainly with its longer neck, long pointed centre tail feathers and its striking markings it is a very graceful bird. It is almost as widespread as mallard though it tends to fly greater distances on migration. They are medium sized ducks which fly fast and high, often dropping very steeply from a good height when coming into their resting or feeding area. It is a highly prized table bird, and its combination of sporting qualities, its abundance and its table potential make it perhaps the second most important waterfowl species after the mallard.

In contrast to these two species, whose population ranges also extend over Europe and Asia, the baldpate or American wigeon is very much a bird of the 'New

World'. The breeding range extends from Alaska through the Prairie provinces of Canada to the mountains and high plains of mid-western United States. In fall they move south and generally spread towards the coast so that in winter they may be found as far afield as Washington and Florida. They are very much birds of shallow water, particularly if there is good grass or grain nearby, as they are grazers much in the same way as some of the geese.

The remaining species of surface ducks that are important to the hunter include both green and blue-winged teal, the shoveller, and the Carolina or wood-duck. The first three of these are widespread on the North American continent though they do not feature in the hunter's bag as often as the species previously described. This is probably due to the fact that large concentrations of these species do not occur as often as the others and, though they have widespread ranges, they have particular environmental preferences which restrict their local movement. The teal are fond of small water flashes and reed bed river margins, while the shoveller's specialised feeding technique demands areas of soft mud and silt. Nevertheless, they are very sporting birds; the teal's rate of climb is legendary, and despite its ungainly looks, the shoveller is a fast and direct flier.

The wood-duck is rather different. There are two pockets of population of this colourful duck, one in the Washington and Oregon coastal area, and the other in the south east states. It is the least migratory of all the duck species, preferring to remain in its woodland and river habitat throughout the year. Its flight is twisting and erratic and it is prized as a table bird. Forest clearance and over hunting have much reduced its numbers, but modern conservation measures have improved the status of this species and hunting is allowed on a restricted scale.

Diving Duck

Five species of diving duck are considered to be prime quarry species for the waterfowler. These include the greater and lesser scaup, the canvasback, the redhead, and the ring necked duck. Both species of scaup migrate for long distances, the lesser spreading southwards from their breeding areas in central Canada, and the greater heading towards the west coast from its Arctic breeding grounds. Where their populations overlap they are difficult to tell apart, as their appearance and behaviour is similar. Their habit of high-speed close formation flying makes them difficult targes and, like the other diving ducks, they decoy well and are good table birds.

The canvasback is proably the all-time favourite diving duck. During the winter it is a bird of the estuaries and coast, although its breeding grounds are well into the continent's interior. It is the heaviest and largest of the divers and is often quoted as being the fastest in the air. Like the baldpate and blue-winged teal it is solely a North American bird, and it is one of the most important duck for the coastal wildfowler on the Atlantic seaboard.

By way of contrast, the ring-necked duck is mainly a freshwater bird, its favourite habitat being swamps and streams in well wooded areas. It is the smallest of the divers, averaging around 1 pound 10 ounces (737 g), and it has a preference for rather shallower waters than any of the other species in this group. They tend to fly in loose flocks, and their ability to make rapid changes of direction make them difficult targets. The last in this group, the redhead, ranks second only to the canvasback as a sporting bird. It is the most widespread of the group and quickly adapts itself to a wide range of aquatic environments. Reclamation and clearance of their breeding grounds in parts of the mid-western states and southern Canada has caused a decline in numbers, and this necessitated the establishment of a number of large waterfowl reserves in these areas, and certain hunting restrictions for this species.

Geese

Overall, the duck hunter in North America has a rich variety of species to hunt, and each species will present different types of target which can, and often do, test his skill to the utmost. Even so, wild goose hunting is often considered to be the ultimate of waterfowl sports, and there are three goose species that are most usually hunted. The Canada goose, whose size depends on the race of bird encountered, ranging from the giant Canada, weighing up to 10 pounds (4.5 kg) to the cackling Canada at about 3 pounds (1.36 kg) is certainly the best known and most widely distributed of the geese. Their natural wariness makes it a real achievement if the hunter's tactics brings him within range of the birds, and their fast flight makes them a testing target. The larger races, particularly, are often missed behind because their size makes their flight appear deceptively slow.

Although they are often treated as separate species, the lesser snow goose and the blue goose are conspecific. Their wintering areas are centred along the Gulf coast westwards from the Mississippi delta and they are very much birds of the Mississippi and central flyways. A number of the lesser snows also use the Pacific flyway, wintering in the west coast states from Washington to California, though land reclamation and over hunting have depleted this population. The greater snow goose, a much larger bird, is confined to the Atlantic flyway, wintering in a rather restricted coastal zone from Maryland southwards. Lesser snow and blue geese average about $5\frac{1}{2}$ pounds (2.5 kg) and reach speeds of over fifty m.p.h. in level flight.

The white fronted goose is perhaps the wildest and wariest of all North American waterfowl. Like the lesser snow and blue goose, it is primarily a bird of western North America, wintering mainly on the Texas and Louisiana coast and in the central valley of California. Unlike the other geese, however, it also occurs in a wild state in Europe and Asia. Its wildness and speed gives it a very high ranking as a sporting bird, and it is also rated highly as a table bird.

These then are the major North American waterfowl quarry species, although other species can assume equal importance in certain specific areas. For instance, the goldeneye is hunted on the shores of the Great Lakes and along the ocean coasts of the continent, the cinnamon teal is important in the south west, and the brant goose is hunted along the west coast of Canada and the U.S.A. With such a great number of species hunted in such a variety of environments, the hunting methods reflect these variable factors, though they can be crystallised into three main techniques. These can be called decoying, pass shooting and jump shooting.

Decoying

Most wildfowl species are gregarious birds and will be attracted by a pattern of decoys laid out to entice them. This attraction is made even stronger if the hunter is also expert at calling in his birds. Shooting is done from some form of hide or blind, though this varies considerably with the terrain and available cover. Timber shooting in Arkansas, where the hunter wades the flooded valley-bottom woodland and uses only tree trunks for concealment, is the simplest form of blind shooting, though to be successful the hunter has to know how to place his decoys to best advantage and to be able to call duck in from quite long distances.

Decoys can also show great variations, from white newspaper laid out on grain stubble to attract snow geese, to artistic masterpieces. The only principle is, if it attracts birds use it! Wildfowl shooting over decoys is the most popular of all duck and goose hunting methods, and the style of gun to use depends to a great extent on personal preference and the shooting situation. Most shooting, however, takes place at ranges greater than is usual in upland shooting, so the guns are normally more heavily choked and tend to be more heavily built to take the express and heavier load shotshells that are more popular for these species. Decoying these birds is only possible in places where they can be reasonably expected to land, that is, at their resting grounds or feeding grounds. Where these two areas are some distance apart, or are inaccessible to the hunter, the second type of shooting is often employed.

Pass Shooting

Pass shooting means intercepting birds as they flight from one area to another and, as in Britain and Europe, the main wildfowl movement takes place in early morning and late evening. At such times a hunter placed underneath a flight line can enjoy very fine shooting. Again a blind of some kind is used in order to conceal the hunter, though some landscapes make concealment difficult. The pass shooter is often presented with higher and faster flying birds than the decoy specialist, and it is in this style of hunting that the magnum duck guns really come into their own. These are guns designed to swing smoothly rather than for quick pointing, they have long barrels, can handle the heaviest loads and are tightly choked to throw good, close patterns of large shot. A magnum in the hands of a novice can, however, be a nightmare. All too often this type of hunter has an exaggerated idea of the gun's range and far too many long shots result in far too many crippled birds. Experienced gunners, on the other hand, can put forward many reasons why the 10 bore is such an effective weapon for the larger species of geese, and it is in a pass shooting situation where one sees most of these big guns being used.

Jump Shooting

Finally, jump shooting is the wildfowling equivalent of the upland shooter's walk-up and flush technique, although in duck hunting it is more often 'creep and crawl up' rather than walk! An area in which waterfowl are known to be is approached to within gun range before the birds are flushed. This can be done on land or by boat, and numerous 'sneak boat' techniques have been evolved in different parts of the continent. As in upland game shooting, the gun used in this sport really needs to be quick pointing, as the flushed waterfowl do not present more than a second or two of shooting opportunity, but choking often remains on the tight side of modified, in order to retain a killing pattern further out.

INTRODUCED GAMEBIRDS

Of all the gamebird species that have been introduced into the North American continent over the last 200 or so years, only three have really become established to the extent that they are now considered to be important quarry species. Thus the ring necked pheasant, the chukkar and the grey or hungarian partridge have added to what was already a rich game bird and wildfowl variety.

The pheasant is, without doubt, the most important of the three, with a wide ranging wild breeding stock which has colonised much of southern Canada and all the U.S.A. apart from the extreme south and south-east. It is a bird having a preference for mixed woodland and farmland which supports a mixture of arable crops and pasture. It has, therefore, occupied its own ecological niche without competing with native game birds.

The chukkar partridge, in size mid-way between the quail and the grouse, originated from the arid hills of the Mediterranean coast, and has found a somewhat similar environment towards the west of the continent. Nevada, Idaho and Wyoming are the 'headquarter' states for this bird, though California, Washington, and Colarado also hold a good wild stock.

In contrast to this, the Hungarian or grey partridge prefers the cooler climate of the North Central states and the prairie provinces of Canada. It is a bird that thrives on open farmland where, like the pheasant, it does not compete with any native species. Both species of partridge have a very low and rapid flight which seldom follows a straight line; the flushed pheasant, on the other hand, 'towers' or climbs rapidly in a frantic effort to gain safety before levelling out to a long glide. Wild birds of these three species are hunted in the normal upland manner, over flushing dogs with a variable number of hunters participating, using the type of guns described previously.

At this point, the breeding of the pheasant and chukkar, particularly in the growing number of Hunting Preserves, should be mentioned. These areas are managed in such a way that birds of these species are bred and released in suitable habitat so that they can be hunted by visiting gunners. These preserves are growing rapidly in popularity, as they can offer sport which in many instances is better than that which the wild birds can provide. Certainly, for the visiting shooter it is an easy and convenient way of sampling some of the continent's best pheasant, partridge and quail shooting.

GROUND GAME

As in Europe, ground game is usually regarded as rifle quarry, although small animals can and often are hunted with shotguns. Species of the rabbit family can, therefore, figure in the shotgun hunter's bag providing he has access to suitable hunting grounds, but even so, shotgunning for ground game is often considered very much a second rate sport. There is, however, one exception. Hunting deer in heavy cover, be it brush or deep forest, has caused the evolution of a special kind of shotgun, designed to handle large buckshot or rifled slug most efficiently. In such an environment, hunters of, say, the white-tailed deer would probably choose an automatic or pump-action 'slug gun' bored improved cylinder in a very short barrel. This shotgun is usually equipped with rifle-style sights and even tapped for a scipe mount. With such a weapon it is possible to group very closely at 50 yards (46 m) and it is often accurate at about 100 yards (91 m) — much further than the woodland deer hunter is ever likely to need. Though bearing a far greater resemblance to a rifle (it is sometimes called, rather unkindly, the poor man's deer rifle) the slug gun can also be used very effectively in close-range bird shooting such as quail or woodcock hunting. One additional advantage this shotgun has over the rifle in this close-range deer hunting concerns the safety factor. The carrying power of a charge of buckshot or a rifled slug is much less than the bullet from any medium velocity rifle, although the heavy weight of the shotgun's load matches a rifle's 'knock-down' power when used against soft skin animals like deer at these ranges. Nowhere else in the world has the shotgun evolved into such a specialised weapon for use against large ground game.

CONSERVATION AND ACCESSIBILITY

The tradition for hunting in all its forms is very deeply rooted in the history of the colonisation of the North American continent, and when hunting pressures begin to seriously cut the population of various species of game, enlightened conservation has sought to redress the balance. Canada and the U.S.A. lead the world in their approach to integrated shooting and conservation, and thankfully, despite much political pressure, hunting for sport is still considered a part of every American's birthright. Sporting organisations like **Ducks Unlimited**, the **National Rifle Association of America** and the **National Shooting Sports Foundation** have a powerful collective voice in the political arena, but their main task is at grass roots level, preserving the habitats that contrast as markedly as the Yukon and Florida, which provide space for the waterfowl, gamebirds, and ground game of the continent to maintain their populations.

From the high tundra of the north to the everglades and deserts in the south, North America contains a wide variety of environments which, in turn, support a wide variety of gamebirds and waterfowl. What makes it even more attractive is that this variety of shotgun sport is generally more accessible to the visitor than in any other part of the northern hemisphere. For the visitor to the continent perhaps the simplest entry into shotgunning would be through one of the game preserves, where a day's shooting can be easily arranged. There are a great number of these preserves which can offer such species as quail and turkey in addition to the more usual pheasant, mallard, and chukkar, so that wherever one stays on the continent, there is probably a preserve nearby. The advantage of these preserves is that shooting can often be arranged at short notice, whereas rather more advance notice is required to shoot the other upland game species and waterfowl on Hunting Club grounds. With a little advance preparation, however, many hunting clubs can show a wealth of variety in the sport they can offer the visitor, and these can be contacted through the national organisations mentioned above, to which they are affiliated.

Generally speaking, most of the sporting rights in North America are in private hands but acquiring permission to hunt is on a far less formal basis than in Britain or Europe. Certainly, access to private land demands some degree of local assistance and tact, but it is normally far more freely available than one is used to on the east side of the Atlantic. As with the other chapters in this section, I have included in the Appendix a list of North American addresses which may provide the springboard into a new type of shooting in a different but exciting environment.

Wherever you go for your shotgun shooting, be it in Britain, Europe or in the New World, I wish you good luck!

*   *   *

APPENDIX

USEFUL ADDRESSES

Major shooting organisations, government bodies, and other sources from which information may be sought:

SHOOTING IN BRITAIN (CHAPTER 6)

Two associations cater for the 'live bird' shooter with the first mentioned serving the interests of all shotgun users in Britain.

National Association for Shooting and Conservation (Formerly WAGBI)
Marford Mill, Rosset, Clwyd, LL12 0HL

British Field Sports Society,
59, Kennington Road, London, S.E.1

Other valuable information may be obtained from:
The Game Conservancy,
Burford Manor, Fordingbridge, Hampshire

For those wishing to rent a period of top quality shooting in the British Isles, there are many organisations through which shooting can be arranged. Among the best-known are:

Cowley and Fell Sporting Agency,
Cree Cottage, Woodland Head, Yeoford, Crediton, Devon

Major Neil Ramsey and Co.,
Farleyer, Aberfeldy, Perthshire, PH15 2JE

Craigroy Sporting Co. Ltd.,
Wiliam Street, Nelson, Lancs.

SHOOTING IN EUROPE (CHAPTER 7)

1. Spain

All information on shooting areas, importation of weapons, and the availability of shooting permits is obtainable through:
The Spanish National Tourist Office,
London

Centrehurst Ltd.,
8–10, Parkway, London, NW1 7AA

Instituto Nacional para la Conservacion de la Naturaleza, (ICONA)
Madrid

In addition to these, a number of estates cater for shooting parties and offer driven partridge shooting of the highest quality. One of the most notable of these is:

Cacerias Tojo Estate (run by Tom Gullick)
Quevendo 13, Villanueva de los Infantes, Ciudad Real, Spain

2. France

The most useful address I found is:

French Government Tourist Office,
178, Piccadilly, London, W1V 0AL

3. West Germany

Importation regulations and shooting permits are issued through:

Embassy of the Federal Republic of Germany,
23, Belgrave Square, London W1V 0AL

Other sources of information are:

German National Tourist Office,
61, Conduit Street, London, W1R 0EN

and the German Hunting Association:

Deutscher Jagdschutz Verband,
Vereingung der dt. Landesjagdverbande, Schillerstrasse 26, D–5300 Bonn

4. Norway

The government department controlling shooting sports is:

Direktoratet for Vilt of Ferskvanfiske,
Trondheim

Other sources are:

The Norwegian National Tourist Office,
20, Pall Mall, London, SW1Y 5NE

and the hunting association:

Norges Jeger og Fiskerforbund,
Hvalstadasen 7

5. Poland

Arrangements for shooting in Poland may be made through:

The Polish Travel Office (ORBIS),
313, Regent Street, London, W1R 7PE

Polorbis Travel Ltd.,
82, Mortimer Street, London, W1N 7DE

Further details through the Polish Hunting Association:

Polski Zwiazek Lowiecki,
00–029 Warsaw, Nowi Swiat 35

6. Hungary

Like Poland, Hungary offers many opportunities for shotgun sports. Visiting arrangements may be made through:

Danube Travel Agency Ltd.,
6 Conduit Street, London, W1R 9TG

Full details of the type of shooting available from the **Hungarian Shooting Bureau:**
Mavad, 1014, Budapest, uri utca 39

SHOTGUNNING IN NORTH AMERICA (CHAPTER 8)

In the U.S.A., the governing body for shooting, from which information may be obtained is:

U.S. Department of the Interior,
Fish and Wildlife Service, Washington D.C. 20240

Other sources are:

The National Rifle Association of America,
1600 Rhode Island Avenue, N.W. Washington D.C. 20034

The National Shooting Sports Foundation Inc.,
1075 Post Road, Riverside, Connecticut 06878

Ducks Unlimited Inc.,
PO Box 66300, Chicago, Illinois 60666

For more information on hunting preserves, contact:

North American Game Breeders and Shooting Preserve Operators Association Inc.,
Goose Lake, Iowa 52750

BIBLIOGRAPHY

Akehurst, R., *Sporting Guns and Rifles*. Bell & Co., England.

Arnold, Richard, *Automatic and Repeating Shotguns*. Barnes & Co., New York.

Greener, W.W., *The Breech-Loader and How to Use It*. Cassel & Co., London.

Gresham, Grits., *The Complete Wildfowler*. Stoeger Publishing Co., New Jersey.

Nadaud, J., *La Chasse, Et le Gibier de nos Regions*. Le Livre de Poche, Paris.

Ogilvie, M.A., *Wild Geese*. Poyser & Co., England.

Puchalski, T., *Bron Srutowa i Technika Strzelania*. P.W.R., Warsaw.

Purdey, T.D.S. & J.A., *The Shot Gun*. A. & C. Black, London.

Rice & Dahl, *Game Bird Hunting*. Harper & Row, New York.

Sedgwick, Whitacker, Harrison, et al., *The New Wildfowler*. Herbert Jenkins, London.

Soothill and Whitehead, *Wildfowl of the World*. Blandford Press, England.

Sprunt and Zim, *Gamebirds*. Golden Press, New York.

In addition to the above, I have made frequent use of various editions of the *NRA Hunting Annual* and *Guns Illustrated*.

INDEX